VINTAGE
Graphic Design

Steven Heller & Louise Fili

VINTAGE
Graphic Design

Type, Typography,
Monograms
& Decorative Design
from the Late 19th &
Early 20th Centuries

ALLWORTH PRESS
NEW YORK

SVA
NYC

ACKNOWLEDGMENTS

We would once again like to thank Tad Crawford, founder and publisher of Allworth Press, for his continued support and for urging us to do a companion edition to *Vintage Type and Graphics*. Gratitude to Chamois Holschuh, our editor on this project. We are grateful to Andy Anzollitto, senior designer at Louise Fili Ltd, for his commitment to the design details of this book.

Finally, a warm thanks to David Rhodes, President of the School of Visual Arts, New York, for his encouragement and enthusiasm.

SH & LF

Allworth Press books may be purchased in bulk at special discounts for sales promotion, corporate gifts, fund-raising, or educational purposes. Special editions can also be created to specifications. For details, contact the Special Sales Department, Allworth Press, 307 West 36th Street, 11th Floor, New York, NY 10018 or info@skyhorsepublishing.com.

24   5 4

Published by Allworth Press, an imprint of Skyhorse Publishing, Inc. 307 West 36th Street, 11th Floor, New York, NY 10018.
Allworth Press® is a registered trademark of Skyhorse Publishing, Inc,® a Delaware corporation.

www.allworth.com

Copublished with the School of Visual Arts

Cover and interior design by Louise Fili and Andy Anzollitto, Louise Fili Ltd.

Library of Congress Cataloging-in-Publication Data
Names: Heller, Steven, compiler. | Fili, Louise, compiler. | School of Visual Arts (New York, N.Y.)
Title: Vintage graphic design : type, typography, monograms & decorative design from the late 19th & early 20th centuries / Steven Heller & Louise Fili.
Description: New York : Allworth Press, an imprint of Skyhorse Publishing, [2020] | Includes bibliographical references.
Identifiers: LCCN 2019030431 (print) | LCCN 2019030432 (ebook) | ISBN 9781621537083 (trade paperback) | ISBN 9781621537090 (epub)
Subjects: LCSH: Graphic design (Typography) | Printers' ornaments. | Type ornaments.
Classification: LCC Z246 .H447 2020 (print) | LCC Z246 (ebook) | DDC 686.2/2--dc23
LC record available at https://lccn.loc.gov/2019030431
LC ebook record available at https://lccn.loc.gov/2019030432

Print ISBN: 978-1-62153-708-3
eBook ISBN: 978-1-62153-709-0

Printed in China

Introduction

IT SHOULD BE A MAXIM ON THE FIRST PAGE OF EVERY DESIGNER'S MENTAL RULE BOOK THAT OUTRAGEOUS TYPOGRAPHY DRAWS ATTENTION TO ITSELF rather than the message. "Type well used is invisible as type, just as the perfect talking voice is the unnoticed vehicle for the transmission of words, ideas," wrote Beatrice Warde, the respected printing historian, in "Printing Should Be Invisible," her oft-quoted essay on legibility published in *The Crystal Goblet: Sixteen Essays on Typography*. Addressing printers, typographers, and designers, she cautioned that "your wildest ingenuity can stop people from reading a really interesting text." Nonetheless, this rule of typographic practice is fraught with exceptions.

When Warde wrote this, she was first and foremost critiquing the challenges to conventional readability of typography triggered by typo-experimentation occurring throughout Europe during the early twentieth century known as "The New Typography." Like many traditionalists, Warde was loyal to the classical tenets of type and, among other taboos, reproached the mixed marriages of old and new styles as acts of typographic hubris. "Printing [which includes typography] demands a humility of the mind," she warned, "for the lack of which many of the fine arts are even now floundering in self-conscious and maudlin experiments. There is nothing simple or dull in achieving the transparent page. Vulgar ostentation is twice as easy as discipline." Referring to the "stunt typographer," Warde granted that although there was a curiously special place in the world of design for "ugly" typography, beauty is the ultimate virtue. However, beauty is really a matter of taste, altered by time and context, and not everyone will agree on what is and is not beautiful.

If typographic apostasy was bitterly attacked by conformists, nontraditionalists needed to aggressively challenge the status quo from time to time. It was a necessary tool, since different kinds of design problems require varied typefaces to solve distinct problems, and sometimes these faces are weirdly idiosyncratic. Good typography cannot always be a crystal goblet; typefaces can be the message, not the vessel. Transparency (or invisibility) does not apply to all designed media. In advertisements, billboards, posters, or signs, garish type design has long captured the eye and excited the senses. Today's digital visual world is filled with graphic design that would drive Warde apoplectic. Typographic styles transform with more rapidity than ever, so describing a typeface with the words *au courant* or *passé* is no longer as useful as when typography evolved at a slower pace. Typefaces and typographic ornament from historical periods—intricate or austere, produced in wood or metal—are assets when used well, not just for nostalgic impulses, but because designers have the need for a wide range of diverse options. Vintage luster adds a charm and personality that cannot always be found in more austere modern faces.

Many of the decorative designs heralded in this book were produced relatively late in the history of type; however, they derived from earlier models of Renaissance calligraphy. As R.S. Hutchings noted in his *A Manual of Decorated Typefaces*—which includes sections on inline, outline, shaded, three dimensional, stencil, cameo, halftone, two-color, and embellished designs: "Their original sources were the copy books of the professional writing masters, at first engraved on wood and later on copper; and—during the nineteenth century—the commercial lithographic artists." These were not intended nor were they perceived as ugly. Decorative faces were "generally well conceived and represented admirable virtuosity of hand engraving," added Hutchings, "They were ingeniously and consistently embellished in a wide variety of styles, almost always applied to undistorted basic forms of normal widths and weights."

During the late eighteenth and early nineteenth centuries, there was what Hutchins called a "harvest of fancy types" that had lost its momentum almost as quickly as it had begun. But around the mid-1800s, a period of exuberance was reborn, a rich market was met by type founders that offered a rich continuum of utter novelties. The lithographic method allowed for the brilliant and profane of the ornamented genre, and many faces could also be pirated by means of electrotyping. Embellished display faces were distributed far and wide up until the turn of the century, when the fashion for them slowly but only briefly ended.

The most fertile, though short-lived, period for elaborately decorated vintages is associated with the Victorian era. The early 1800s saw rapid innovation and continuous growth in printing and type technology. The Industrial Revolution had given rise to retail goods, commerce, and the wealth of visual artifacts that comprised mass communication of the middle into the late 19th century. The need to reach a burgeoning consumer class fostered a widespread increase in letterpress printing/

design, which led to a boon in commercial typography. Type foundries in Europe (particularly in Britain) were wellsprings for bold compositions and arresting type design. Mechanical advances, such as electrotype, pantograph, and router, contributed to mass font production that triggered a tidal wave of boisterously decorated typefaces. Although the overarching style is called "Victorian" or "Victoriana" and is distinct to the era of English Queen Victoria (1837–1876), it is not, in fact, limited to the little monarch's lengthy reign or empire. In fact, Hutchins stated "their active lease on life was comparatively short." The production of Victorian typefaces moved in and out of favor throughout different time periods, many of them having been revived for their nostalgic charm and contemporary usefulness by designers much later into the twentieth century.

Nicolette Gray, the English type historian, wrote that type design of this period represented a sense of transition and abandon. "Suddenly, without warning, the insular British craftsman began to use a complicated and sophisticated artistic medium in a way totally foreign to his culture, and used it with verve and subtlety. It is a remarkable phenomenon," she noted " ... the changing moods which are recorded in Victorian type designs are not those of the individual artist, but a reflection of the mood of his society." Typefaces were designed by anonymous employees of founders, whose goal was to supply commercial culture with novelties to corral public enjoyment.

Looking back at their origins, Victorian designs were produced in conditions of a commercial free-for-all and outright piracy. While many Victorian types have been revived by digital foundries today, the sheer number of those done in the style-of has made it difficult to establish their true origins. The types and ornaments herein, however, are definitely the real things from bone fide sources. Many started as drawings that were electrotyped, while others were made into punch cuts, but all were created to fill particular aesthetic needs of the nascent period of graphic design.

Gray, who was famous for her 1938 book *Nineteenth Century Ornamented Types and Title Pages*, said: "[N]ineteenth century typography has certain advantages over other arts. It is not so sensitive perhaps to changing mood as that most detailed of all records of fashion, costume design, but it can be more alive to us than the faded silks of our ancestors." As we put forth here, type is free from the tyranny and dominance of any particular style—at least in today's free-aesthetic-realm. This book is not a history, but a delicacy, yet it is important to pay homage to Gray's thinking behind her book. She attempted to indicate "the characteristic intonation of the design, and its connotation in the psychological complex of the years of its invention and vogue."

The typefaces she praises and criticizes are more or less among those selected here from various foreign sources—although not all vintage type is of an ornamented kind.

As type gourmets, the authors savor historical and historically inspired type in many forms—especially the aesthetically idiosyncratic and the printed artifacts on which historical typefaces are sampled. If you are also a type enthusiast, you will doubtless derive joy from the letters and ornaments culled from the rare and forgotten sources we have reproduced herein. If you are as enamored by the quirky and the sensual, you will take pleasure from the pure joy of seeing these rediscovered sample pages.

This is not a history book, but rather a collection of tasty confections—so-called eye candy. Yet the rationale for producing an entirely new, full color volume as a companion to our original 2011 black-and-white book, *Vintage Type and Graphics*, is not just for delectation for its own sake, but to show beyond a drop shadow of a doubt that just because a typeface or decorative device is old does not mean it is old fashioned.

Much of what has been chosen for inclusion both reflects and satisfies our mutual tastes for early and mid-19th to early 20th century eccentricities in printing material, including stock pictorial cuts, filigree borders, and cartouches galore. For decades, we have scoured the antiquarian book and flea markets of Paris, Berlin, Rome, Florence, Barcelona, and elsewhere online and in auction catalogs to find examples of graphic design that is worth preserving and reviving in our books. We have collected aesthetic gems from numerous historic typeface catalogs and specimen sheets from the eras when craftsmanship was at its zenith and attention to manufacture was rigorous. These beautiful (yet often absurd) rarities once played a key role in advertising, publication design, and sign painting professions. They represent the quirky and peculiar fashions from distinct moments in popular art when they were first produced. These are like typographic bulls in the proverbial china shop. They broke many of the rules of classical type design, and, to continue a mixed metaphor, they are to type what costume jewelry is to jewelry—ostentatious yet magnificent.

Decorative Letters

DECORATIVE AND ORNAMENTED TYPEFACES WERE DEVELOPED IN THE EARLY NINETEENTH CENTURY. Advertising replaced itinerant tradesmen as the primary hawker of goods. "Early in the nineteenth century, English type founders produced a variety of embellished types designed to emphasize their unique characteristics for the single purpose of attracting attention." Alexander Lawson, in *Printing Types: An Introduction*, wrote: "Fat faces, grotesques, and Egyptians—decorative types when compared to the Romans that had undergone but minor changes since fifteenth-century Italy—were not flamboyant enough for the new requirements of advertising display." Type founders discovered a wide market for advertisements and package designs and soon shifted from altering existing faces to creating more unequaled inventions. Letterforms mimicked the appearance of Gothic architecture and were intricately and extravagantly designed. Some of these alphabets were reproduced from letters found in ancient manuscripts; others were conceived by known and unknown artists. An important distinction must be made between ornamented typefaces and "fancy faces," since designers of the latter were prone to derive inspiration more from common sign painters than from monastic manuscripts. An 1879 issue of the *Typographic Advertiser* said, "We change, tastes change, fashions change. But fashion's rule is despotic, and so, yielding to her commands, we have prepared and show in this number some oddities to meet the taste of the times. ... As printers desire to be in fashion, we trust they will approve our course by sending in orders for them, that their patrons also may catch the infection..."

1

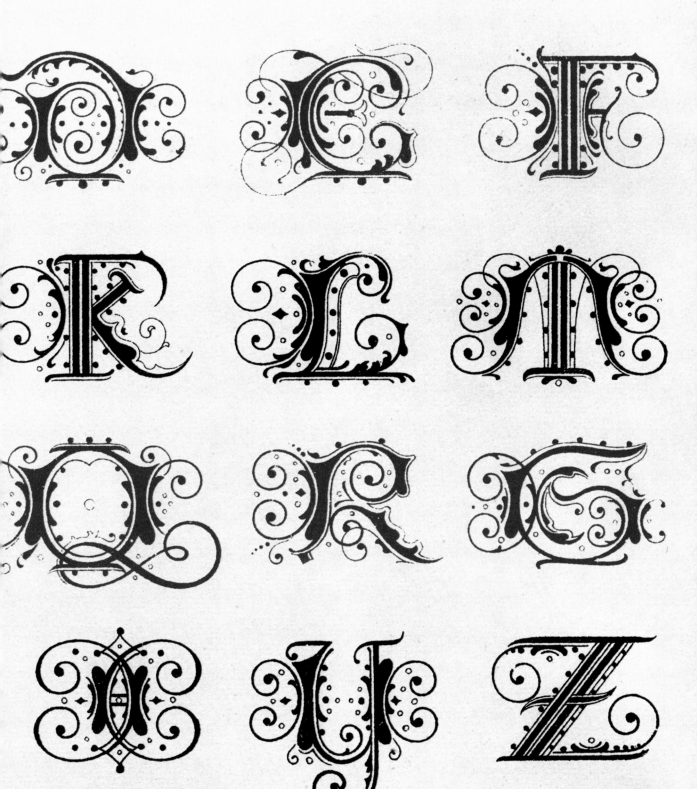

I . V
D

6

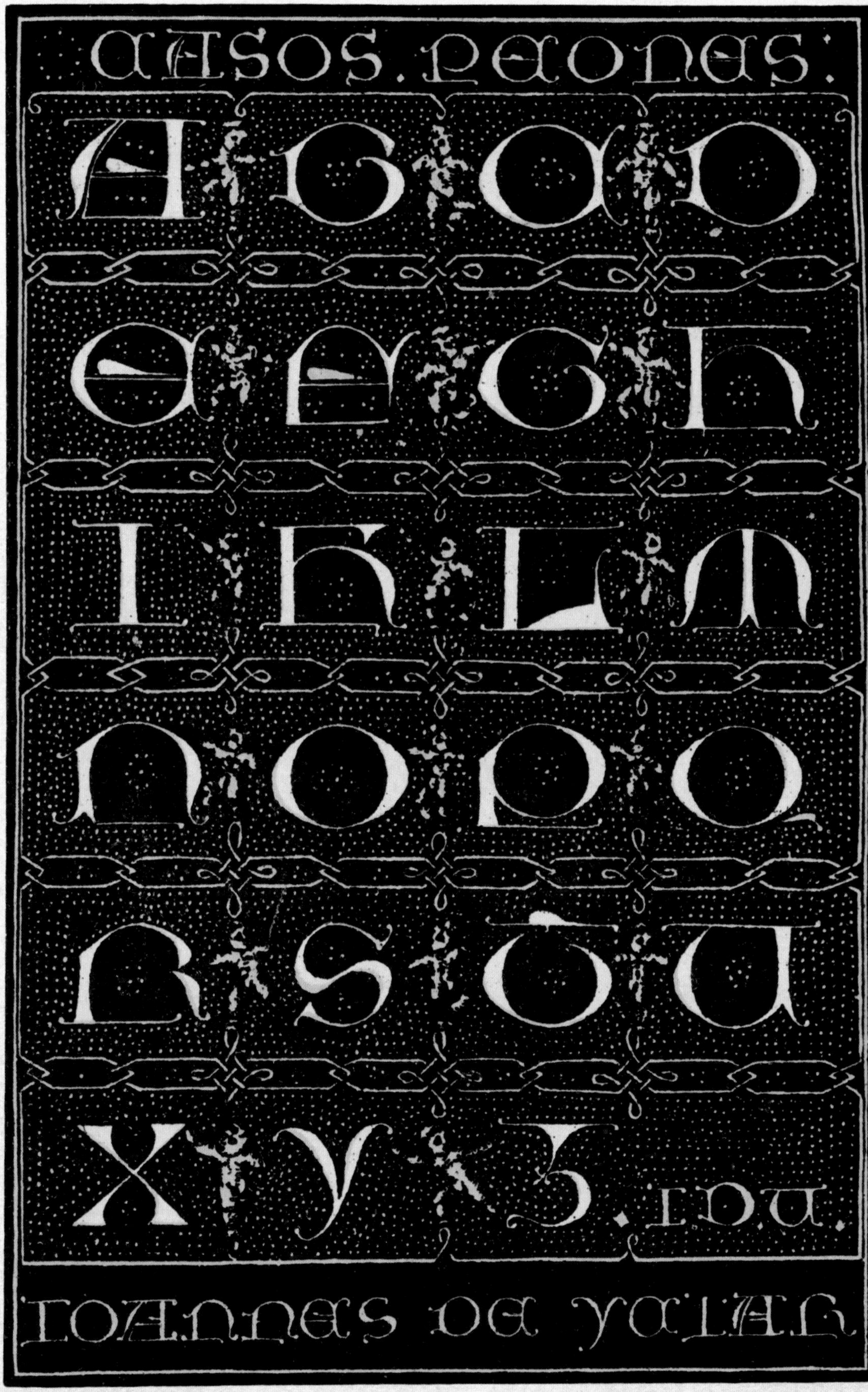

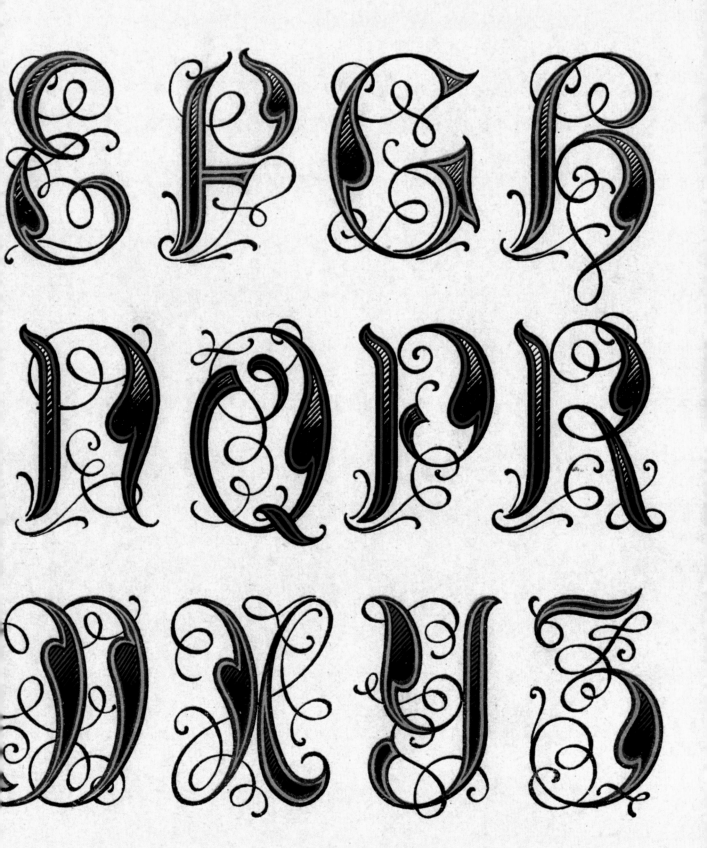

11

12

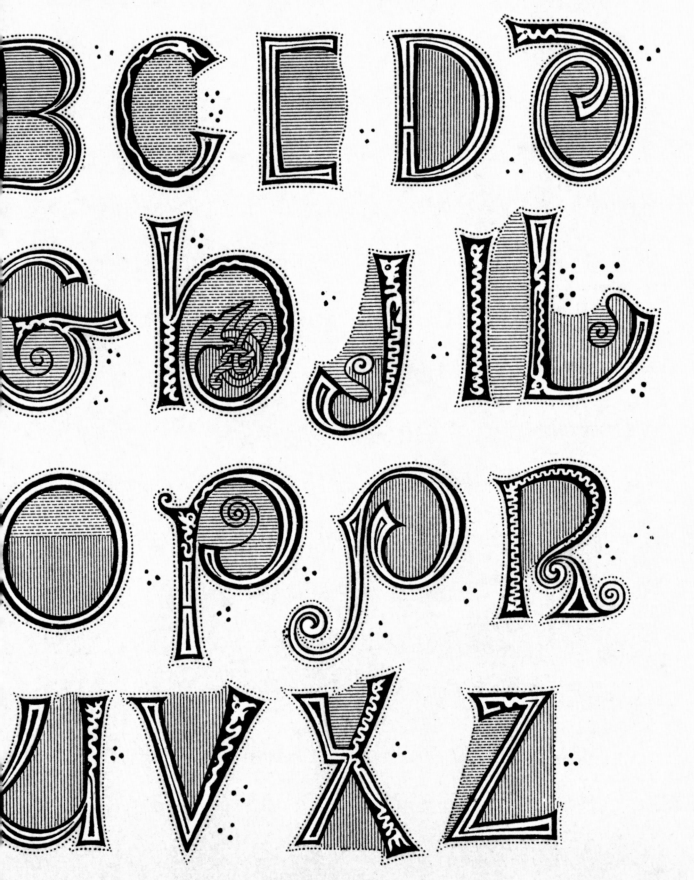

ingefasst. (||||| rot ▓▓ blau ▒▒ gold).

13

14

15

16

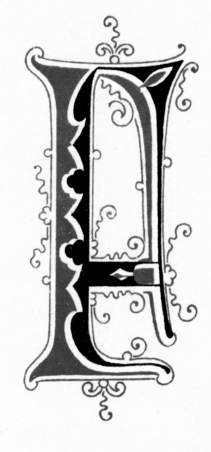

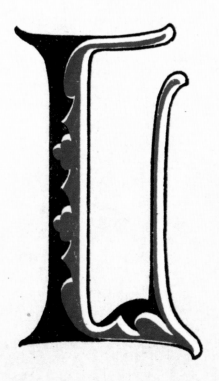

21

AABCD GHHHK PQRRST ·18

DEEEF

LMNNO

VVXYZ

93.

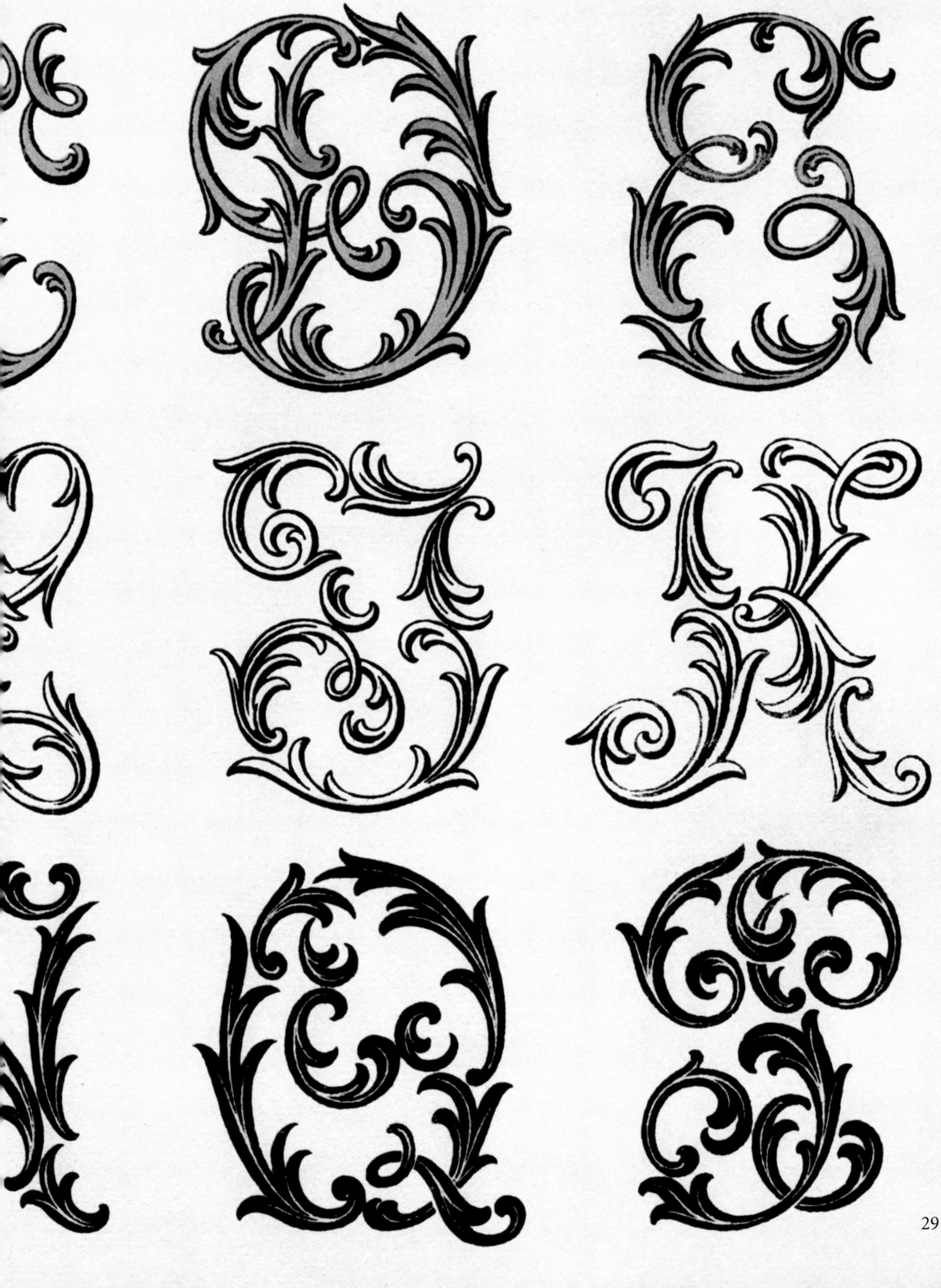

ABCD
JKLM
STUV

EFGHI

MNOPR

WXYZ

ABCD
JKLM
SZUV

E F G H

N O P R

W X Y Z

ABCD
HJKL
RSTV

43

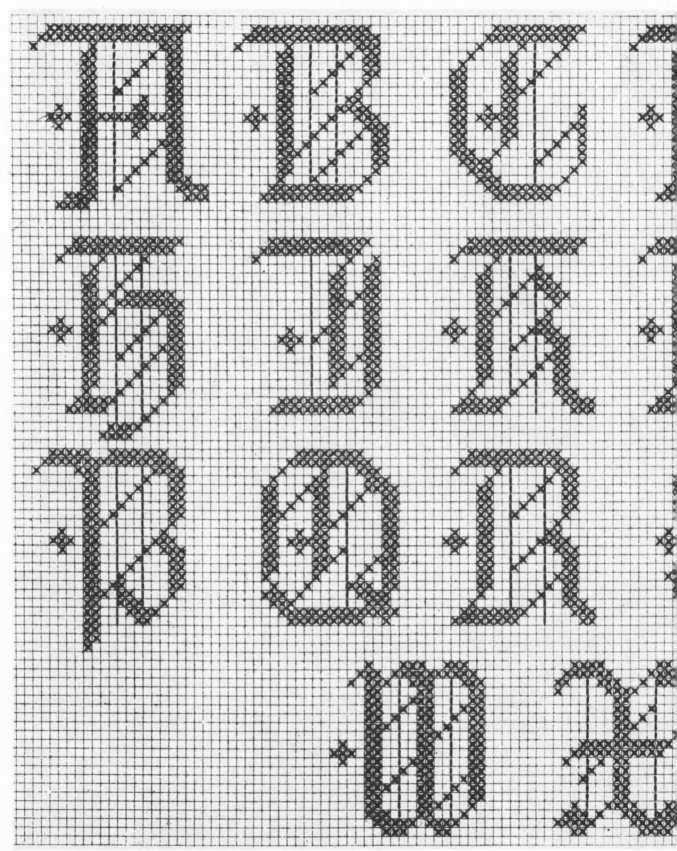

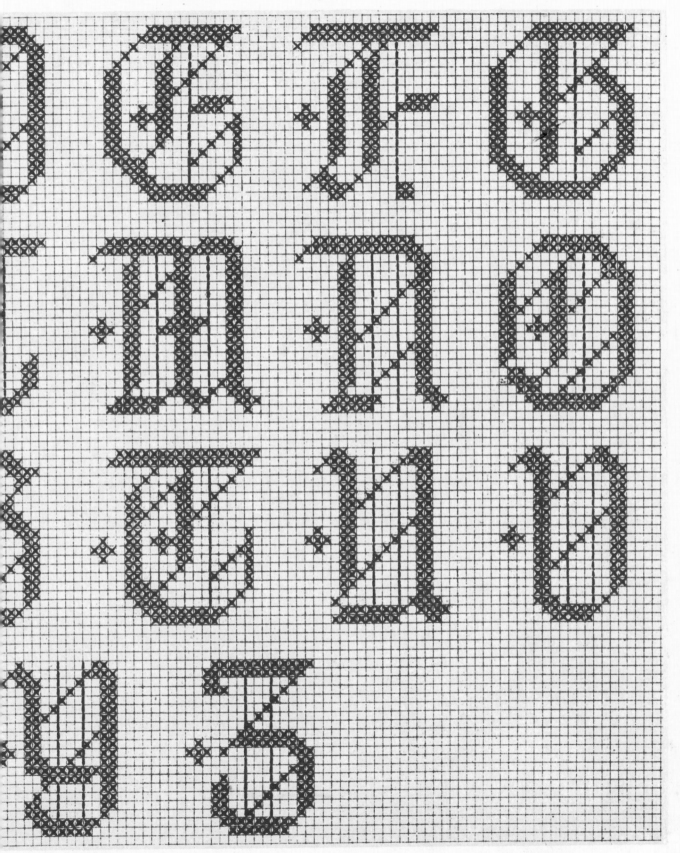

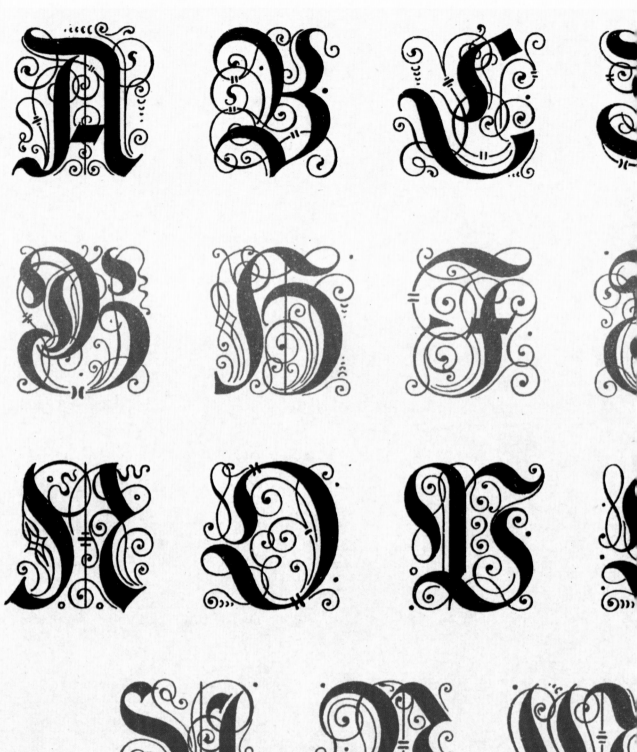

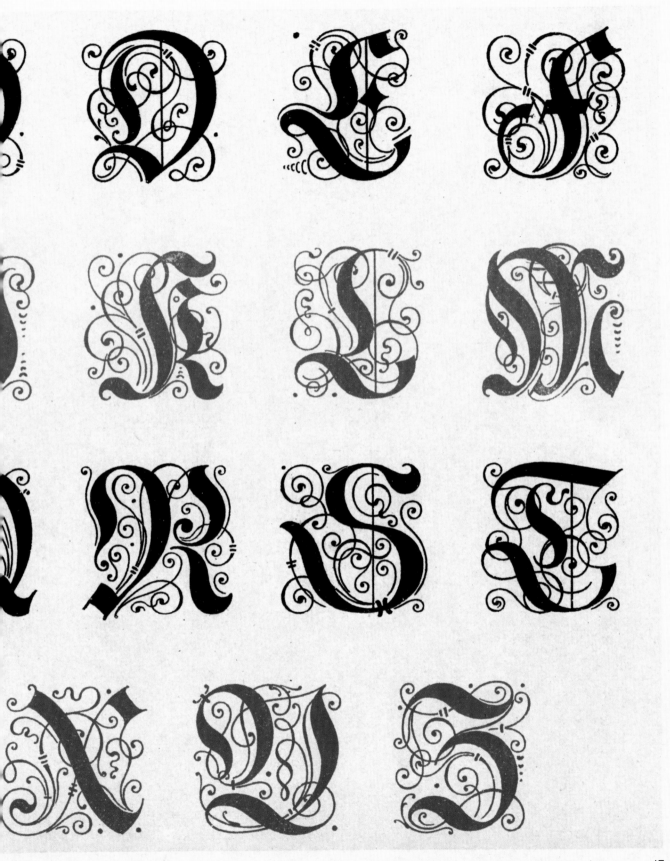

47

A B C D

K L M N

S T U V

a b c d e f g h

r ſ s t u

F G H I

O P D K

W X Y Z

k l m n o p q

w x y z

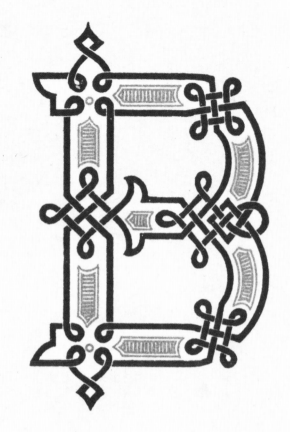

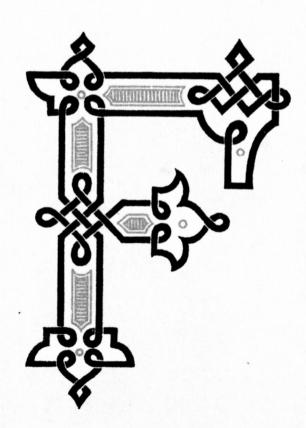

Philippicus
Seculo
verschwend
und ließ dur
Thracien u

wurde im Achten

omiſcher Kaißer,

te die Reichsgüter

h die Saracenen

s Aſien verwüſten.

54

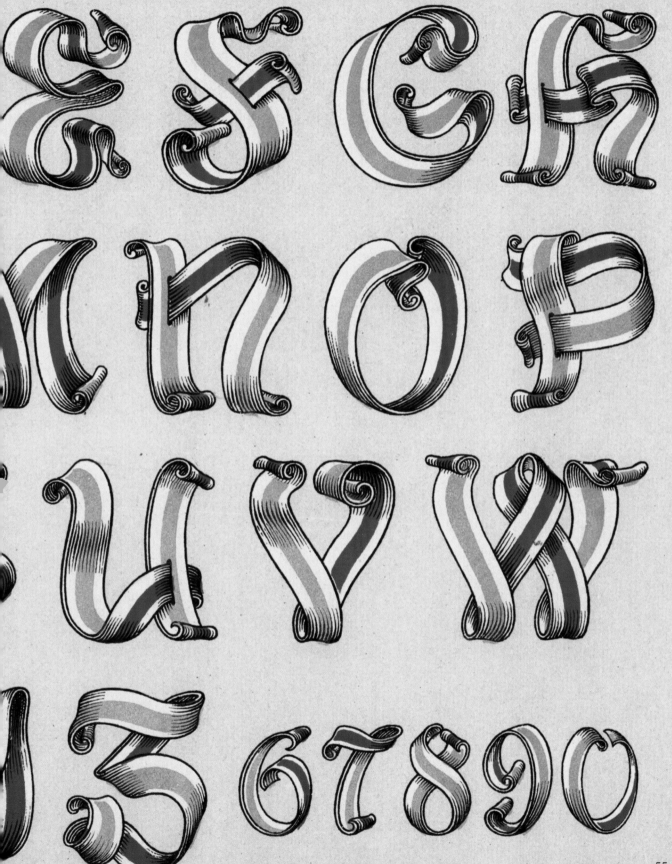

A B C
G H J
N Q P
U V W

D E F

K L M

R S T

X Y Z

ABCDE
KLMNO
TUVW
12345

FGHIJ

OPQRS

XYZ

67890

AVIATIO

DÉCORA

Cyclisme. Athlet

PUBL

CIVILE

TION BIG.

me.Football.ect

CVTÉ

ABCDE
MNOPQR
YZ 55 1234
ABCDE
KLMNO

GHIJKL
STUVWX
567890 XVIII
FGHIJ
PQRST

63

Ornament

IN ADOLF LOOS'S 1908 ESSAY "ORNAMENT AND CRIME," THE AUSTRIAN ARCHITECT ARGUED, "THE EVOLUTION of culture marches with the elimination of ornament from useful objects." Design had been stuck in an ornamental quagmire. After the 1896 blossoming of Art Nouveau, forests of twisted vines, stems, and tendrils—a floriated madness—covered everything from books, magazines, advertisements, posters, and typography to clothing, furniture, and buildings. Loos's preference for "smooth and precious surfaces" derived from his belief that objects swathed in ornament were guaranteed instantaneous obsolescence. Yet visual austerity might be seen as a denial of aesthetic pleasure. Who would argue that a miniature ornamented Persian manuscript or *The Book of Kells*, with its interlocking patterns and serpentine filigree, is not among the most beautiful artifacts? How could Baroque and Rococo motifs in two and three dimensions be pilloried for crimes against the eye? Ornament was not a veil to hide ugliness; it was an antidote to dreariness and monotony. Ornamental embellishment is not inherently evil, even in excessive doses; sometimes excess is divine. Nonetheless, passions are inflamed when the topic of ornamentation is injected into matters of design. The Bauhaus rejected Art Nouveau ornamentation as symptomatic of a bourgeois aesthetic tyranny. Followers of the Bauhaus and adherents of orthodox Modernism, even to this day, have maintained the belief that minimalism enables the clearest communication—and purity is transcendent. Graphic complexity does not diminish communication. Yet even a tasteful garden needs care and a good pruning from time to time.

Ott-Heinrich-Bürgerschule
Mairimwald i Steiermark

American
Bar ₂ Café
USA

JAMES SHMITH

DURESCO
THE KING
of water
paints

THE SILIKATE PAINT COMP.
CHARLTON ₂ LONDON · S·E·

HOEHL

SEC
extra
DRY

MIG

Münchener
Neueste
Nachrichten

2 AUSGABEN
TÄGLICH

FUCHS
SÖHNE

Spedition
und Möbel
Transport
Düsseldorf

PIANOS

12 UNTER DEN LINDEN
BERLIN & BOSTON U·S·A·

ORGELN

WILKINSON & HEYWOOD & CLARK & VARNISHES LONDON BANNER-STR 58 60

TRADE MARK

'ENRICO. 'IBOSSOS. 'FABRICA. 'MERCI DI. METALLO. 'NAPOLI.

1501

MIG

ESTABLISHED 1862

B. WILLIAMS TOY-BAZAR NEW-YORK.

TOYS DOLLS GAMES & NOVELTIES

NUR EIN PREIS

GOLDENE
ISAAK KOHN
3 MK-BAZAR
MARKTPLATZ 9

NUR EIN PREIS

THEE SALON MIKADO

DIE GANZE NACHT OFFEN

MAISON DUVALI OBJETS D'ART MEUBLES & BIJOUX

POSTAMT 4

B. GANZ & CO MAINZ "MANUFAK-TUR" FÜR VORHÄNGE TEPPICHE & MÖBEL-STOFFE

Eugen Xander

Bier-~~
Brauerei
zum
gegr: 1625

Otto Dämblich

Antiquitäten
Kupferstiche
Bilder Möbel
Fayencen
Broncen
Stoffe

Nouveau Cirque

Ant: Baregi
Südfrüchte/
Obst/Eier/
Geflügel &
Wildbret

Fische

Landschafft=
& Handels=
Gärtnereiß
des

J. Wulff junr.

JOS.GEYR
SPORTBUREAU

LONDON
BERLIN
PARIS

BRÜSSEL
DUBLIN
WIEN

ROM·BUDAPEST·NEW YORK·MÜNCHEN·KIEL

MIG

TABAK
COMPAGNIE
BREMEN
- - - - - -
HABANNA
CIGARREN
:·FABRIK·:
GEGR·1842

WEIN
STUBE
NOAH
- - - - -
C·BINUD

ATELIER
ELVIRA
DRESDEN

DAMEN
HERREN
KINDER
MODEN
PARISER
MODELLE

NIEDERLÄNDISCHE
LEBENS·FEUER
UNFALL·DIEBSTAHL
HAFTPFLICHT·VIEH
HAGEL·AUSSTEUER
SCHIFFS·UND REISE
VERSICHERUNGSBANK

HOTEL & PENSION
ROLAND
HONNEFaRHEIN
HAUS ERSTEN RANGES

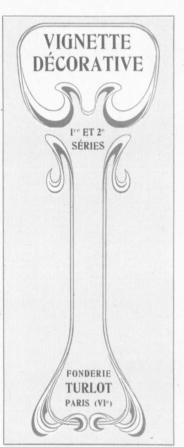
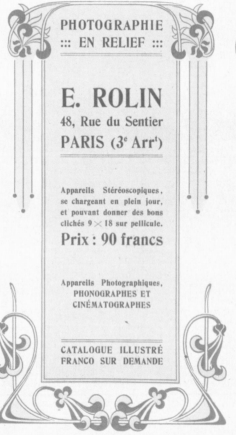

W. RICHARDSON
& SIMONET Frères

CAMÉES ET ÉMAUX
DIAMANTS ET PERLES
AMÉTHYSTES, SAPHIRS
ÉMERAUDES, TOPAZES

24 - 26 - 28
Rue Auber
PARIS

SUCCURSALE
7, Rue du Bac

Les plus beaux   *Les plus riches*

GEORG
SCHÖTTLE
MÖBEL-
FABRIK
STUTTGART
SOLIDESTE
AUSFÜHRUNG
SÄMTLICHER
MÖBEL

LERMOOS
AM FUSSE DER ZUGSPITZE
HOTEL & PENSION
DREI MOHREN
VORZÜGLICHE KÜCHE
MÜNCHNER BIERE
TIROLER WEINE
FISCHWASSER
M. JÄGER

MÄSSIGE
PREISE

DECKEN
UND
WÄNDE
FÜR DAS
MODERNE
HAUS
VON
M. J. GRADL
24 FOLIOTAFELN
IN FARBDRUCK
PREIS
-M. 26.-

AUFGANG
ZUR
GALLERIE

COMPTOIR
VON
PAUL MAUR

DER MODERNE STIL

MODERNE BAUFORMEN
MONATSHEFTE FÜR ARCHITEKTUR
PREIS DES GANZEN JAHRGANGS 12 HEFTE M. 24.- IN MAPPE M. 26.-

JULIUS HOFFMANN
VERLAG, STUTTGART

AUSSTELLUNG MODERNER GEMÄLDE

Menu

Preis-Verzeichnis

Tanz-Karte

Konzert-Programm

FESTE PREISE

Speisenfolge

LETZTE NEUHEIT

P. S.

CIGARREN & CIGARETTEN
·C·RENARD·

 REIHE 8

 CASSA

 RANG 1

 LOGE 4

MEUNIER FISCHER BLACK & COMPAGNIE

W. SHMIDT SOHN
RASEUR
FRISEUR
COIFFEUR
MANICURE

PASSAGE BUREAU B. MAIER
mig

CAFÉ & AMERICAN BAR:

CAFÉ RESTAURANT INTERNATIONAL

IMPORT EXPORT **V. MARTIN** EN GROS EN DETAIL

ELSE WINTERSTEIN

PUTZMACHERIN

WESTERLAND = SYLT

C. TIMM

MODES

NEUE
KUNST

BAR

CAFÉ

PUCK

FRIED
LADNER
UHREN

OTTO
LOEB

GOLD =
WAREN

R · MÜLLER

RESTAURANT
BAHNHOF
STUTTGART

FRÜHSTÜCK
DINERS
SOUPERS
BELEGTE
BRÖDCHEN

GEMÄLDE SALON
GEÖFFNET TÄGLICH
VON 10-1.U 2-3 UHR

GEÖFFNET EINTRITT
VON 10 — 12 50 PFENNIG
VORMITTAG KINDER
VON 1-3 MILITÄR
NACHMITTAG 30 PFENNIG
AUSSTELLUNG
GIESSEN

MAX FRITZ
TISCHLEREI
SCHILLERSTRASSE

KAKAO
KAFFE
THEES
CHOKO-
LADEN
CONFÜ:
TÜREN

VERLAG
MODERNE

WISSENSCHAFT
TECHNISCHES
DICHTUNGEN
VORLAGE
WERKE
MONATS
HEFTE

The New Gallery

· HIGH · CLASS · PICTURES ·

EXPOSITION
PERMANENTE
DE
TABLEAUX
SCULPTURES
GRAVURES
OBJETS D'ART

GRAND
RESTAURANT
LEDUC

SALONS & CABINETS

VERLAGSBUCHHANDLUNG
J. Hoffmann
· STUTTGART ·

PIANOS
ERARD
STEINWAY
IBACH
GÜNTHER
PLEYEL

ORGUES

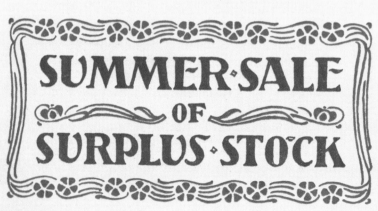

SUMMER · SALE
OF
SURPLUS · STOCK

TENTOONSTELLING
VAN OVDE
SCHILDERIJEN
DER
VLAAMSCHE SCHOOL

DENTELLES
SPITZE
LACES
ENCAJES

G·VANZYPE
MÉLASSE
EN GROS

PRODUITS
DES
FLANDRES

INDVSTRIE · NATIONALE
Solvay & Cᵒ
Huitres & Moules parquées
BLANKENBERGHE · OSTENDE · NIEVPORT

Modes de Sylvie Rose
30   30
Fournisseur de la Cour

Otto Gotha Berlin Kiel

IN DE DREY KONINGEN

⑤

Fox Vins du Rhin et de Hongrie

Sam. Weller
Ship Broker

Arnold
Ladies Taylor

80

CACAO ·· SUCHARD.

MÖBEL·FABRIK

INNENDEKORATION.
MODERN & ALTER STIL

BUCHDRUCK-CLICHES FÜR SCHWARZ- UND FARBENDRUCK

MODERNE MÖBEL- UND TÜR-BESCHLÄGE

GLASMALEREI UND KUNSTVERGLASUNG.

DEUTSCHE TAPETEN UND FRIESE

TEPPICHE UND MÖBELSTOFFE

FABRIK FÜR BELEUCHTUNGS-GEGENSTÄNDE IN JEDER LICHTART

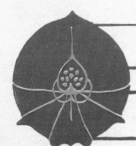

INDISCHE BLUMENSEIFE

Vignette "Dotting Ornament"

A la demande, nous fournissons des **Pièces détachées**

Pour les Prix, voir notre **Tarif général** en cours

DÉSIGNATION DES PIÈCES

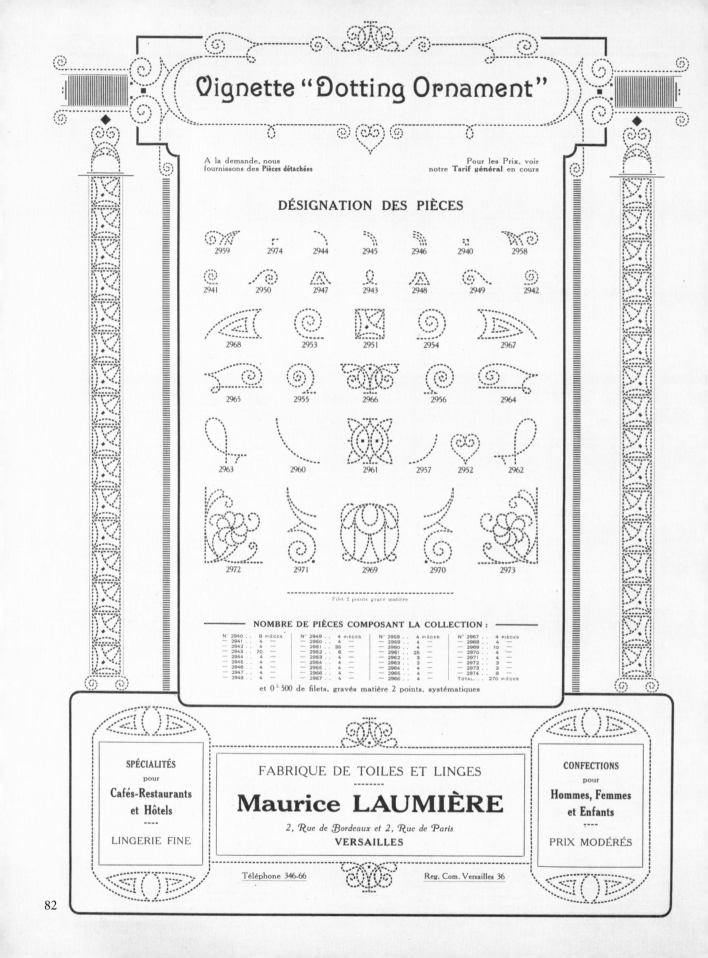

2959 — 2974 — 2944 — 2945 — 2946 — 2940 — 2958

2941 — 2950 — 2947 — 2943 — 2948 — 2949 — 2942

2968 — 2953 — 2951 — 2954 — 2967

2965 — 2955 — 2966 — 2956 — 2964

2963 — 2960 — 2961 — 2957 — 2952 — 2962

2972 — 2971 — 2969 — 2970 — 2973

Filet 2 points gravé matière

NOMBRE DE PIÈCES COMPOSANT LA COLLECTION :

Nº 2940 .. 8 PIÈCES	Nº 2949 .. 4 PIÈCES	Nº 2958 .. 4 PIÈCES	Nº 2967 .. 4 PIÈCES
— 2941 .. 4 —	— 2950 .. 4 —	— 2959 .. 4 —	— 2968 .. 4 —
— 2942 .. 4 —	— 2951 .. 36 —	— 2960 .. 4 —	— 2969 .. 10 —
— 2943 .. 70 —	— 2952 .. 6 —	— 2961 .. 25 —	— 2970 .. 4 —
— 2944 .. 4 —	— 2953 .. 4 —	— 2962 .. 3 —	— 2971 .. 4 —
— 2945 .. 4 —	— 2954 .. 4 —	— 2963 .. 3 —	— 2972 .. 3 —
— 2946 .. 4 —	— 2955 .. 4 —	— 2964 .. 3 —	— 2973 .. 3 —
— 2947 .. 4 —	— 2956 .. 4 —	— 2965 .. 4 —	— 2974 .. 8 —
— 2948 .. 4 —	— 2957 .. 4 —	— 2966 .. 4 —	TOTAL... 270 PIÈCES

et 0 ʰ 500 de filets, gravés matière 2 points, systématiques

Vignette Directoire

A la demande du client, nous fournissons toutes les **Pièces détachées**

Pour les prix de la collection et pièces détachées, voir notre **Tarif général**

DÉSIGNATION ET DÉTAIL DES PIÈCES

Filet simple 3 points n° 1, œil de côté

Filet triple, 6 points n° 1052

Filet double, 3 points n° 593

NOMBRE DE PIÈCES COMPOSANT LA COLLECTION :

N° 1	20 PIÈCES	N° 11	16 PIÈCES	N° 21	6 PIÈCES	N° 31	4 PIÈCES	N° 41	6 PIÈCES
— 2	20 —	— 12	8 —	— 22	4 —	— 32	4 —	— 42	6 —
— 3	20 —	— 13	8 —	— 23	4 —	— 33	4 —	— 43	6 —
— 4	20 —	— 14	8 —	— 24	4 —	— 34	8 —	— 44	6 —
— 5	12 —	— 15	8 —	— 25	4 —	— 35	6 —	— 45	4 —
— 6	20 —	— 16	8 —	— 26	4 —	— 36	8 —	— 46	2 —
— 7	8 —	— 17	8 —	— 27	4 —	— 37	6 —	— 47	2 —
— 8	8 —	— 18	4 —	— 28	6 —	— 38	4 —	— 48	2 —
— 9	8 —	— 19	4 —	— 29	6 —	— 39	4 —	— 49	2 —
— 10	8 —	— 20	4 —	— 30	4 —	— 40	4 —	TOTAL.	374 PIÈCES

et 8 lames de filets matière spéciaux, 3 et 6 points

CASSEAU SPÉCIAL
pouvant contenir cette Collection
Dimensions : 0.65 × 0.44

3124
1 couleur, 10 fr. — 2 couleurs, 15 fr.

3125
1 couleur, 7 fr. — 2 couleurs, 12 fr.

3119
1 couleur, 5 fr.
2 couleurs, 8 fr.

3146
1 couleur, 8 fr. — 2 couleurs, 13 fr.

3147
1 couleur, 6 fr. — 2 couleurs, 10 fr.

3118

84

Galvanos modernes

Galvanos modernes

3117
1 couleur, 8 fr. — 2 couleurs, 14 fr.

3111
1 couleur, 18 fr. — 2 couleurs, 23 fr.

3123
1 couleur, 6 fr. — 2 couleurs, 10 fr.

3151
1 couleur, 6 fr. — 2 couleurs, 9 fr.

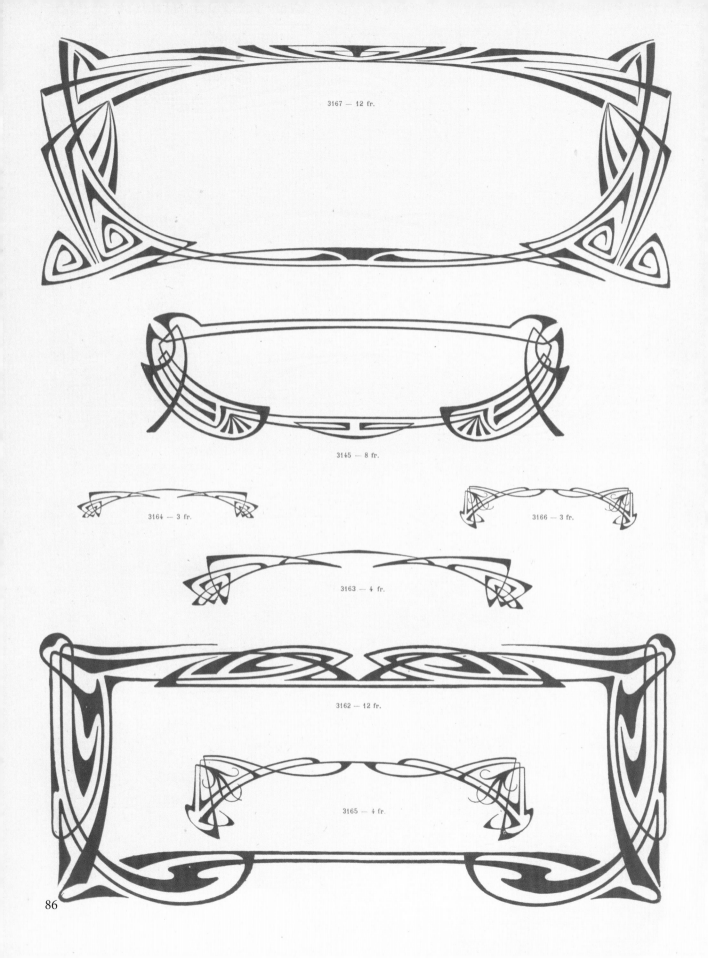

3167 — 12 fr.

3145 — 8 fr.

3164 — 3 fr.

3166 — 3 fr.

3163 — 4 fr.

3162 — 12 fr.

3165 — 4 fr.

3142 — 12 fr.

3085 — 7 fr.

3083 — 7 fr.

3008 — 3 fr.

3002 — 6 fr.

3084 — 4 fr.

3040 — 4 fr.

3006 — 4 fr.

3086 — 4 fr.

87

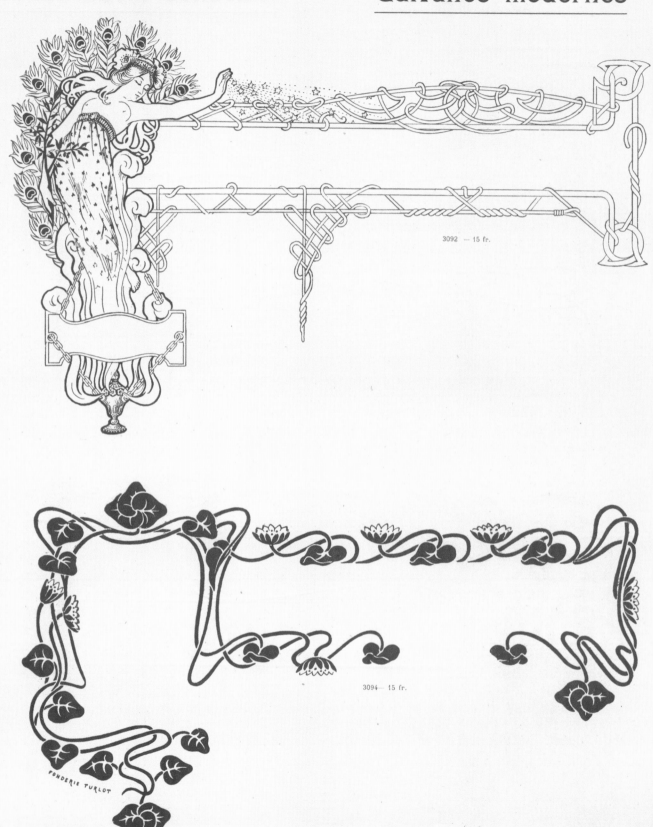

3092 — 15 fr.

3094— 15 fr.

FONDERIE TURLOT

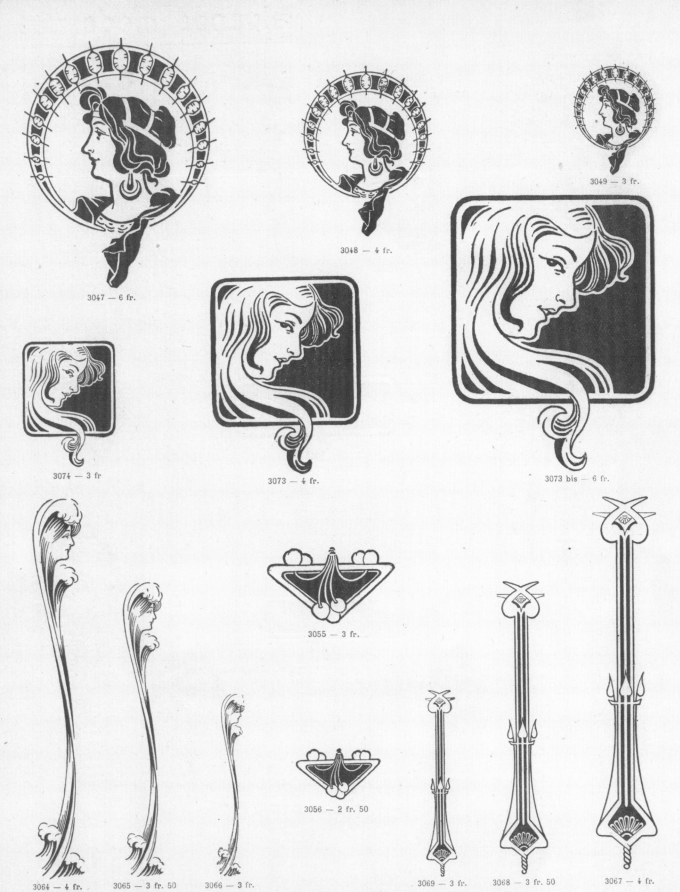

3047 — 6 fr.

3048 — 4 fr.

3049 — 3 fr.

3074 — 3 fr

3073 — 4 fr.

3073 bis — 6 fr.

3055 — 3 fr.

3056 — 2 fr. 50

3064 — 4 fr.

3065 — 3 fr. 50

3066 — 3 fr.

3069 — 3 fr.

3068 — 3 fr. 50

3067 — 4 fr.

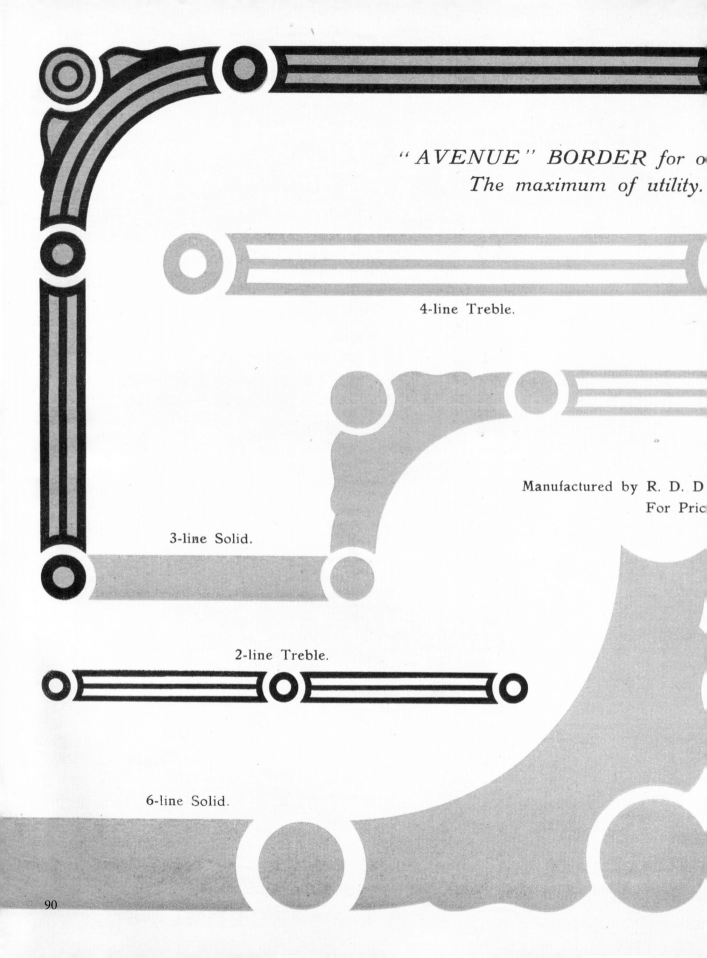

"*AVENUE*" *BORDER* for o

The maximum of utility.

4-line Treble.

Manufactured by R. D. D

For Pric

3-line Solid.

2-line Treble.

6-line Solid.

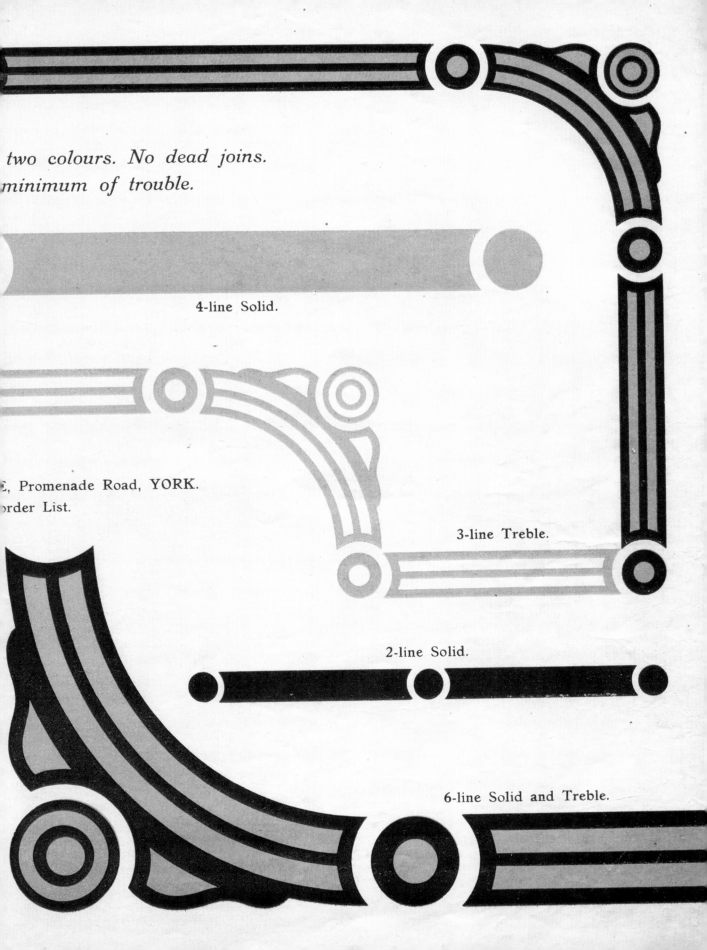

two colours. No dead joins.

minimum of trouble.

4-line Solid.

E, Promenade Road, YORK.

order List.

3-line Treble.

2-line Solid.

6-line Solid and Treble.

ABCDEFG

OPQRST

abcdef

noprst

AUSSTELLUNG

□□□ MODERNER □□□

Zimmer=Einrichtungen

UND

Bürgerliche-Wohnungen

□ zur Besichtigung □
□ ohne jeglichen □
KAUFZWANG

═══ □□□□□□ ═══

A. BAUDOR

MÖBEL-FABRIK

KARL C

Atelier für feinste

Haararbeiten

Franz. engl. deutsche

Parfümerien

GHJKLMN

UVWXYZ

ghiklm

uvwwyz

MBAR

REPRODUCTIONS·
ANSTALT.
N. ROODON

SCHUTZ-MARKE

Grossartige Auswahl
IN FEINEN
Lederwaren
SAMMTLICHE
Reise·Artikel
□□□ solid preiswert empfiehlt □□□

HANI HAUER
:: ZÜRICH 1 ::

Flourishes

LETTERING AND TYPOGRAPHY HAD BECOME ESSENTIAL IN THE DECADES FOLLOWING THE INDUSTRIAL REVolution. The emergent business economy and commercial culture in England, France, Germany, and the United States during the late 19th and early 20th centuries gave rise to a prodigious printing industry. Mammoth type foundries regularly issued new typeface families (some were bastardizations of classic faces) that were touted through elaborate style guides designed to entice the public to consume goods. Business could not exist without advertising. Functional printing types were the core necessity, yet novel typefaces with eclectic personalities were seasonal fashions of the typographic industry. Most of the designs in this book have flourish; those in this section include faces with modishly nuanced details, including elaborate swashes that suggested elegance. Customized lettering, rendered with precision yet elastic in form, ran the gamut from austere to animated, notable for their fluid curlicues and meandering swirls, among other graphic tropes. Many of these typefaces were based on decorous handwriting —scripts influenced by graceful and boisterous pen and brush calligraphy transformed by founders into type metal and wood fonts. Others are one-of-a-kind lettering, drawn especially for a particular advertising display or publication cover and title page. Some are full of character and attitude. Still others were considered by critics at the time to be "perverted monstrosities." Regardless, they represented the times when designed, or, as Nicolette Gray wrote, "Hitherto each type has simply expressed the mood of the moment, or some distinct strain in that mood."

PILKINGTON'S TILE & Pottery Coy, Limited.

TILEWORK & MOSAIC for CHURCHES & other Buildings

CLIFTON JUNCTION near MANCHESTER

TILES OF EVERY KIND for WALLS FLOORS HEARTHS GRATES FUR-NITURE &c. &c.

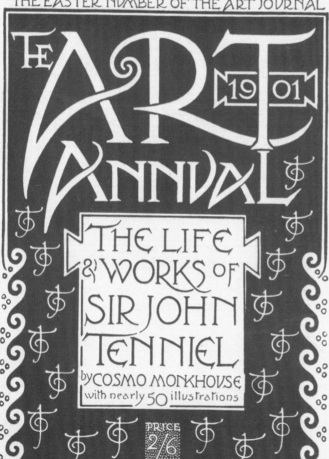

The ART ANNUAL 1901

THE LIFE & WORKS OF SIR JOHN TENNIEL by COSMO MONKHOUSE with nearly 50 illustrations

PRICE 2/6

H. VIRTUE & Co. Ltd. LONDON

SEDDING

ALPHABETS OLD & NEW LTD BTB

Memorandum from 64 JEFFREY & Co. Paper-stainers Essex road, Islington, N.

LETTERING

JOB AND HIS FRIENDS.

Primary Quarterly

Vol. XI.

SECOND QUARTER

APRIL-JUNE

1893

THE AMERICAN

SUNDAY-SCHOOL UNION

1122 Chestnut Street, $ 10
PHILADELPHIA. $ Bible House, NEW YORK.

THE SOCIETY which Takes care of the CHILDREN

CENTURY LITH. CO, PHILA.

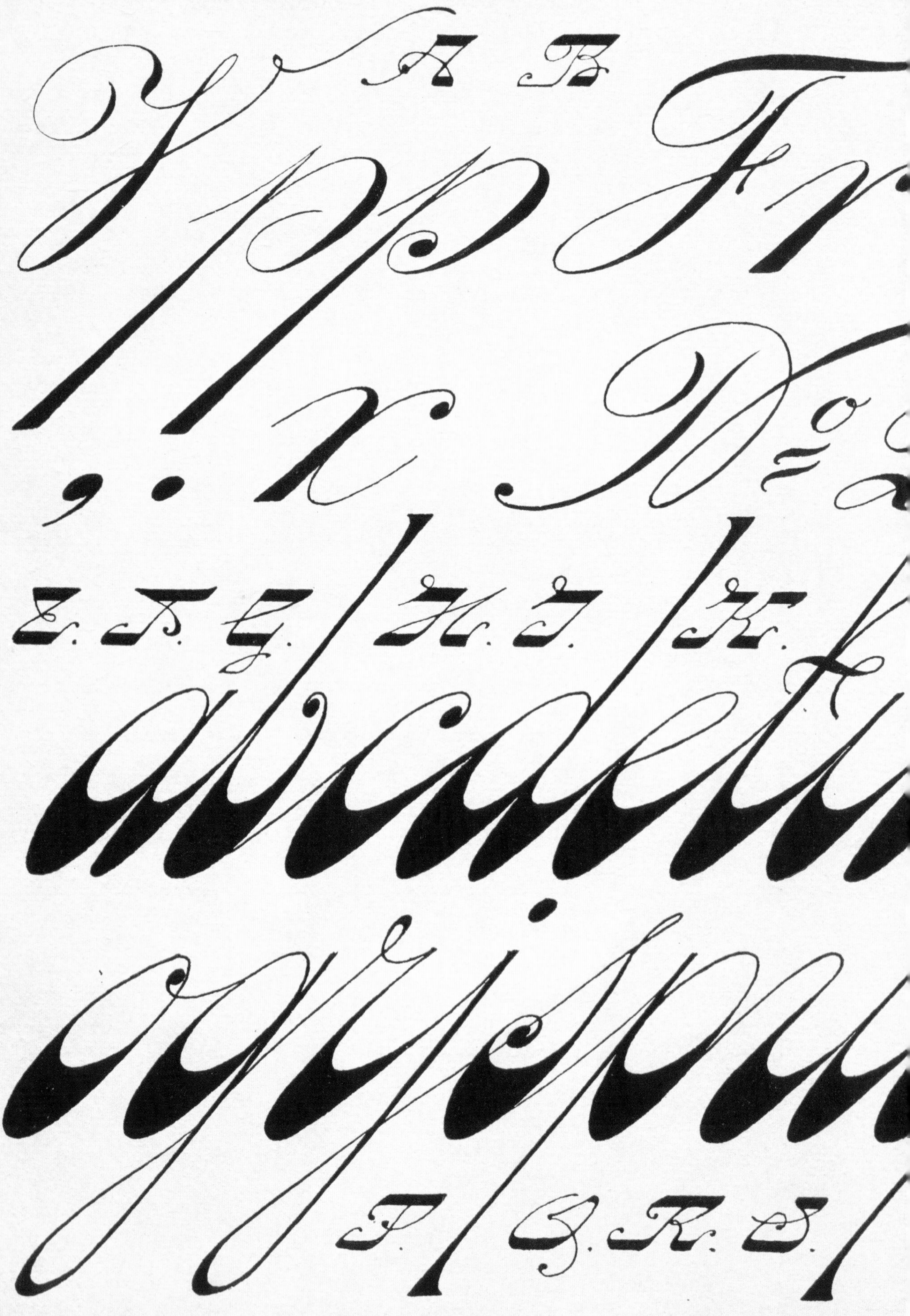

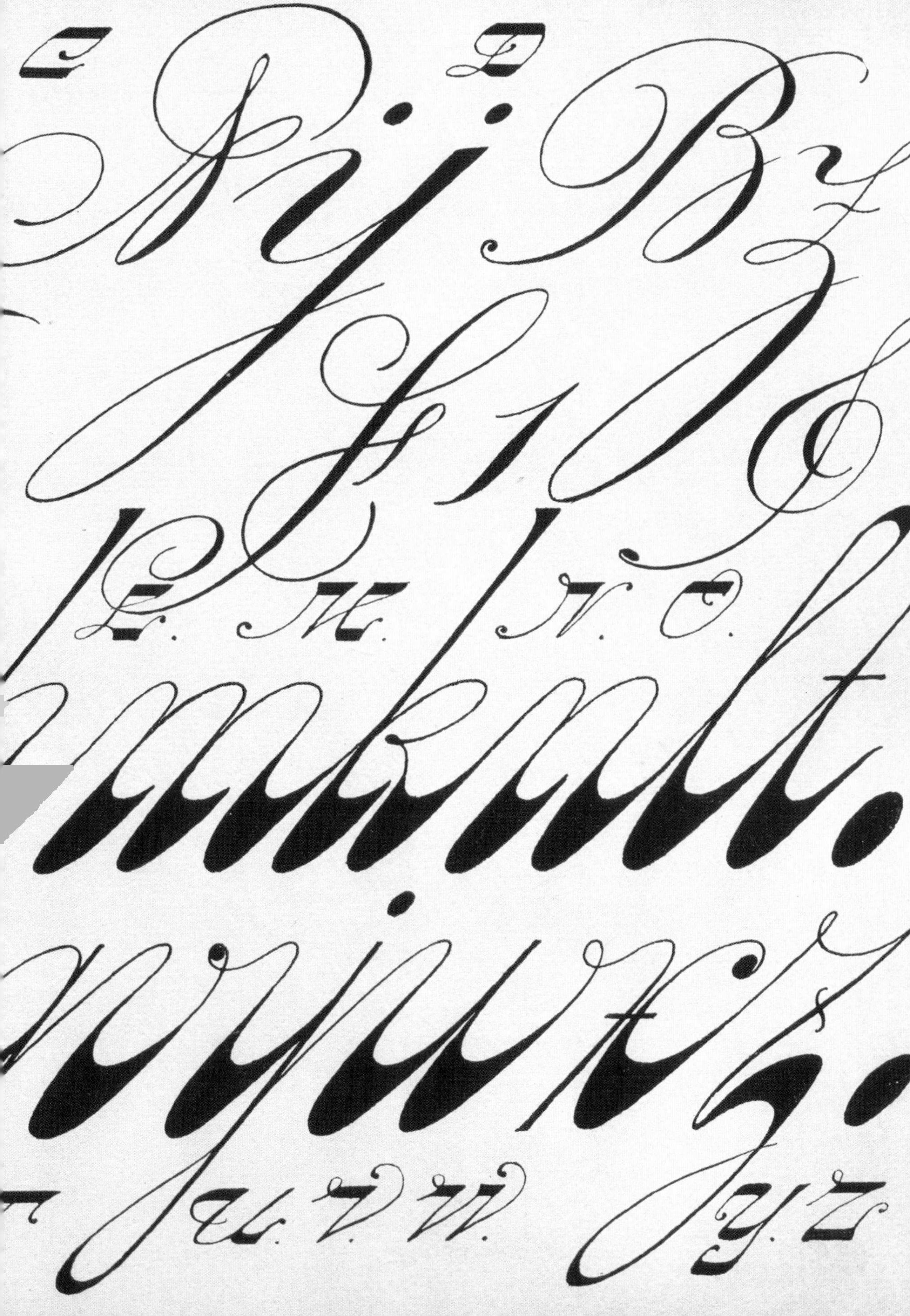

DELITTLE,S "EBOR" SCRIPT.
Prices : double Class 3.
Sizes shown here are 6, 10 and 24-line pica.

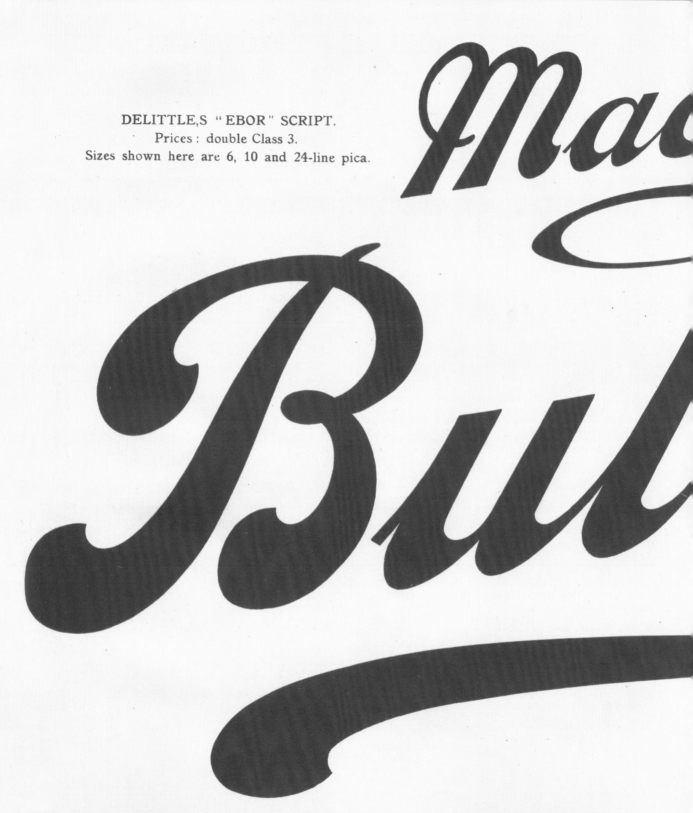

intosh

and

Redmire & Son

A B C D

F K L U

R S T U

Z abcdefg

pqrstuvwxy

Galactina
Kindermehl

Remington
Typ

F G H

N O P Q

U X Y

ijklmno

& *Eckartsberg*
& Cie.

riter *Photos A.G.*
WÄDENSWEIL
AM
· ZÜRICHSEE

BRONZEN
CHRISTOFLE
Bongart jr.
ALFENIDE

103

A B C
D E F 
M N Q R S U
abcdefghijkl
New-York
Paris London
Menu Fritz

R...
Blau
Garte

B

G H I
K L P
U V W X Z
nopqrstuvw

Fahne
rant
tschaft

Café
Restaurant
...zur...
Palme

T. Graham

6-line.

Shadow

8-line.

Down.

10-line.

Eva

12-line.

Concerts

Dance

Code.

House.

Bonds.

20-line.

R. D. DELITTLE, Promenade Road, YORK.

Edwards

12-line.

Terminal No. 1.
Dash No. 3.

Hardy

Limited

16-line.

4-line.

Terminal No. 3.
Dash No. 2.

Ward & Co

8-line.

Terminal No. 2.
Dash No. 4.

DELITTLE'S 20-line "EBOR" SCRIPT.
Prices : double Class 3.

Dean

A B C D

J K L M

S T U V

A B H P B

bcfghj - kmc

F S H J

G P Q R

X Y Z .

R Heldrina

pstuvwxyz.

WIENER GROTESK INITIALEN

Zu Wiener Grotesk und Wiener Grotesk Versal Seite 489 und 489a

3211. Corps 48. Sortiment 11 Figuren (je 2 Stück) ca. 1 kg

A C D E G H
M O R S S

3212. Corps 60. Sortiment 11 Figuren (je 2 Stück) ca. 1,250 kg

A C D E G H
M O R S S

3218. Corps 72. Sortiment 6 Figuren (je 2 Stück)

A E G M R S

ZEILEN-SCHMUCK SERIE 670

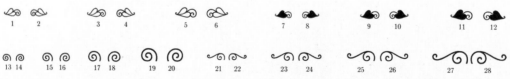

| 1 | 2 | | 3 | 4 | | 5 | 6 | | 7 | 8 | | 9 | 10 | | 11 | 12 |

| 13 14 | 15 16 | 17 18 | 19 20 | 21 22 | 23 24 | 25 | 26 | 27 | 28 |

Sortiment enthaltend je 40 Stück der Fig. 1—4, je 30 der Fig. 5 u. 6
" " " 40 " " " 7—10, " 30 " " 11 u. 12
" " " 50 " " " 13—18, " 40 " " 19 u. 20
" " " 20 " " " 21—28.

Nᵒ 3191. — Corps 9

Tous nos Caractères d'Imprimerie, Modernes
ou Classiques, indépendamment des variations de forme qui les distinguent et aussi

23   REVUES ENCYCLOPÉDIQUES   89

Nᵒ 3192. — Corps 12

Tous nos Caractères d'Imprimerie
Modernes ou Classiques, indépen-

34   GRANDE ASSEMBLÉE   87

Nᵒ 3193. — Corps 18

Le plus court croquis en dit plus qu'un long rapport

52   FONDERIE TYPOGRAPHIQUE A PARIS   39

Nᵒ 3194. — Corps 24

Recommandé pour Travaux de Fantaisie

64   CLASSIQUES & MODERNES   83

Nᵒ 3195. — Corps 30

Manufactures de Tapis Orientaux

7   TOUS LES MODÈLES   5

Nᵒ 3196. — Corps 36

De belles FIGUES vertes 4

Nᵒ 3197. — Corps 48

Ballon ROND avec 8

Nᵒ 3198. — Corps 60

Riche BAIN son 6

Clichés

PREMADE ART MAY HAVE BEGUN IN THE SIXTEENTH CENTURY DURING THE EARLY ERA OF PRINTING WITH engravings that distinguished artisans' book bindings. Most were decorative, including floriated sprays, but eventually this kind of design evolved into representations of creatures and things. In the vernacular of letterpress and lithography, the word "cliché" referred to generic signs, symbols, pictographs, and vignettes used by compositors and printers as repeated spot ornaments, Eventually called "clip-art," ready-made illustration, also known as "cuts," were created by draftspersons working for typeface foundries and commercial art studios. Clichés were available in familiar and unique styles and sold through specimen catalogs. Clichés ran the gamut from ubiquitous all-purpose pointing fingers to more elaborately rendered and witty cartoon characters; from run-of-the-mill scenes and mundane objects to laughing and frowning heads to domestic and wild animals, fruits, and vegetables. Religious and funerary iconography were staples, too. Countless variations were produced for calendars, menus, and all kinds of businesses; to celebrate birthdays, marriages, and holidays. In addition to the garden variety of stand-alone symbols, there were metaphoric and conceptual clichés—realistic, impressionistic, expressionistic. Any theme, style, or mannerism that caught the eye or relieved grey type masses were ripe for cliché. Most were anonymous, yet also some brand names like Conrad X. Shinn (Cobb Shinn), the most prodigious American cut-maker, sold to printers through frequently issued *Cutalogs*. The market for these catered to customers who could not afford original illustrations.

D-1043

B-16

D-1049

D-1044

B-47

D-1050

D-1045

B-46

D-1051

B-45

D-1046

D-1052

B-48

D-1047

D-1053

K-123
A back number

118   D-1048

D-1054

January

D-2776

February

D-2777

March

D-2778

April

D-2779

May

D-2780

June

D-2781

D-2788

D-2262

NELSON WHITE

HD-159

July

D-2782

August

D-2783

September

D-2784

October

D-2785

November

D-2786

December

D-2787

F-779

F-991

F-782

D-2312

F-794

D-2313

D-2314

F-793

D-2315

D-2316

F-799

F-811

D-2317

F-791

F-992

F-777

D-2318

D-1944

D-2320

NO? YES!

F-796

ZOOM-

F-839

TRA-LA-LA-

F-797

HOW-?
WHAT-?
WHERE-?

F-773

D-2319

D-1943

D-2321

121

D-2068

D-2057

D-2030

M E N U

D-1782

M E N U

D-1837

Fountain
SERVICE

D-1790

Listen,
or you'll be sorry!

D-1942

D-1569

D-2069

D A N C I N G

Better come with us!

D-1949

T-1218

D-1781

D-1011

D-2078

D-1017

D-1012

B-812

D-1018

D-1013

B-811

D-1019

D-1014

B-810

D-1020

D-1015

D-1021

D-1016

D-2092

D-1022

123

BLUMEN UND SAMEN
KARL OFER

Karl Slowacik
Tapezierer

HERREN- UND DAMEN-
KLEIDER
KONFEKTIONSABTEILUNG

Konditorei
FRANZISKA RORSHAM

Tab

HERREN=
UND
DAMEN=
KONFEKTION

STEMPEL

LEOPOLD

Trafik

POSTWERTZEICHEN

KONDITOR

FROMMER

...BEREI U.

...PUTZEREI

...FWÄSCHEREI

RADIO

Block Letters

A TYPICAL BLOCK LETTER IS INDEED A BLOCK-SHAPED, ANGULAR LETTERFORM, USUALLY SANS SERIF BUT not always. In fact, for purposes of this section, included here are kindred serif alphabets from *Schriften-Schatz, Eine Sammlung Praktischer Alphabete Für Berufszeige Aller Art* that have a blocky aesthetic presence. Whatever other features it may possess, a block letter has volume, weight, and mass that in some cases result in an illusion of three dimensions. Block letters are indisputably legible and therefore were in frequent use on railroad signs and as newspaper headlines and other forms where instantaneous readability was (and still is) a functional necessity.

A block typeface could be made from metal and wood, or carved into stone. A block letter is not characterized by a drop shadow, inline, or outline, but can include all three design features. A block letter takes the form of a brick or slab and gives a sturdy impression in whatever weight. During the late nineteenth century, block letters were popular as hand-drawn poster faces and designed to capture the eye of the frantic passersby. Block letters are grotesque and neogrotesque, and customized versions are plentiful in specimen books. The block letter comes closest to the ideal of modern typography born in Germany, where the spiky gothic Fraktur was replaced with "grotesk" sans letters set in tight blocks, reminiscent of monumental stone inscriptions. Letters and words were composed at sharp asymmetric angles intersecting other letters and words framed by bold rules and borders that are heavy, massive, and difficult to ignore. Block letters were (and are) the workhorses of clear display.

ABGD
JKLM
RSTUV

SCHRIFT.

EFGHI

NOPQ

WXYZ

131

ABCDE
KLMNO
TUVV

abcdefg
opqrstu

F G H I J

O P Q R S

V W X Y Z

h i j k l m n

v w x y z

133

abcde
lmnop
vw
12345

fghijk

nrsut

xyz

67890

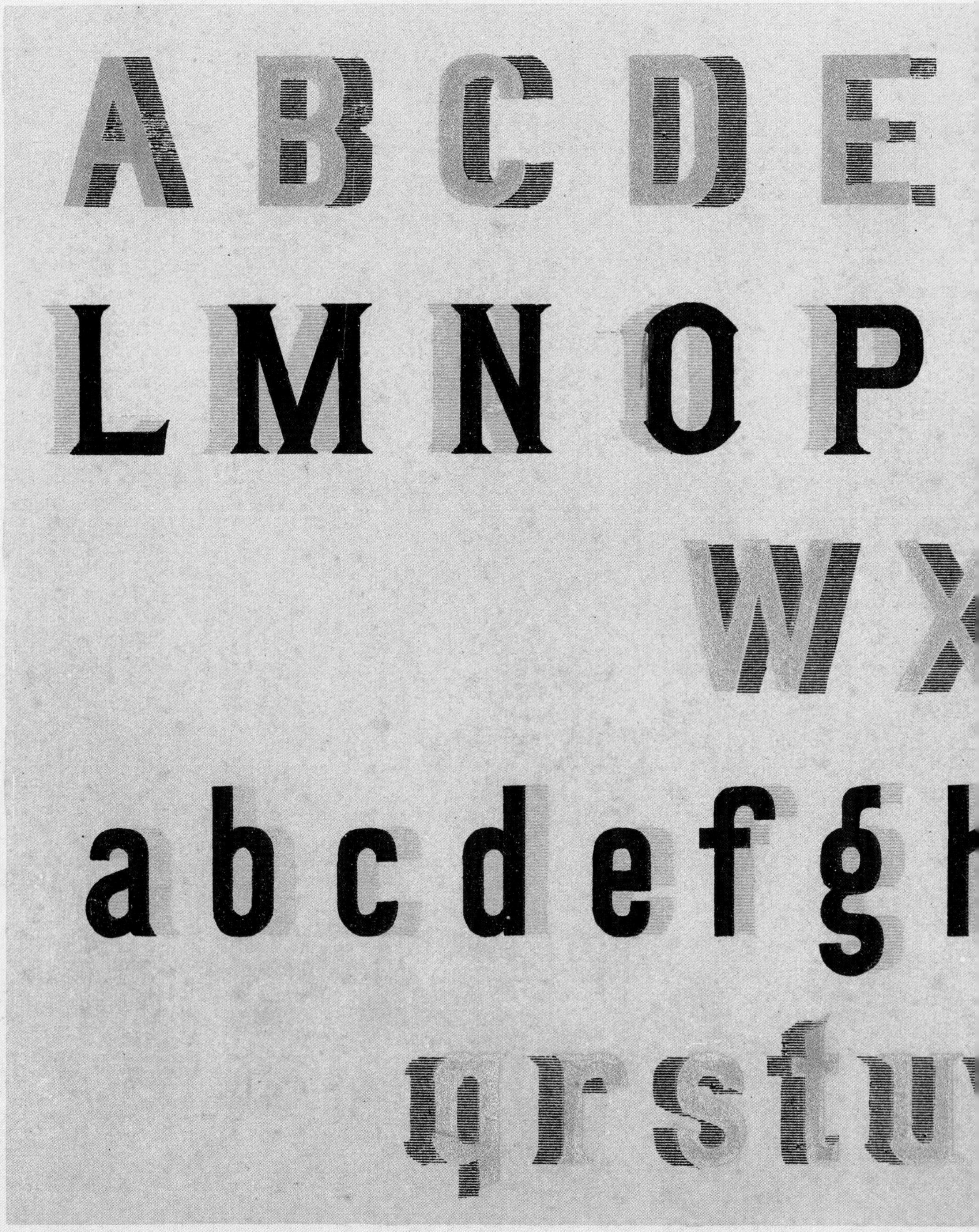

A B C D E

L M N O P

W X

a b c d e f g h

q r s t u

F G H I J K

O R S T U V

Y Z

i j k l m n o p

W X y z

ABCDE

IKLMN

STUVW

EFGHIJ

OPQR

WXYZ.

SCHATTEN-SCHRIFT

CHROMO

1563 a. Corps 32. Min. ca. 6 kg

KURHAUS TAMBACH
SAISON-NEUHEIT

1564 a. Corps 42. Min. ca. 7 kg

WEBER & HEINZE
HAMBURG

1565 a. Corps 48. Min. ca. 9 kg

MODEHAUS

1566 a. Corps 54. Min. ca. 10 kg

BAD NAUEN

Von vorstehender Schrift können kleinere Quantitäten nicht abgegeben werden
Ausgabe für einfarbigen Druck siehe Schattenschrift Seite 394 n und Fette Secession Versal Seite 394 m

ABCDEFG
HIJKLMNO
PQRSTUV
WXYZ‡

abcdefghijk
lmnopqrsſʄ
tuvwſyʒʦ?

MEXIC

LTPVH

MARC

OBFG

KZ8Y.

UISE

SCH

HELFT

KON.

JK OST VW

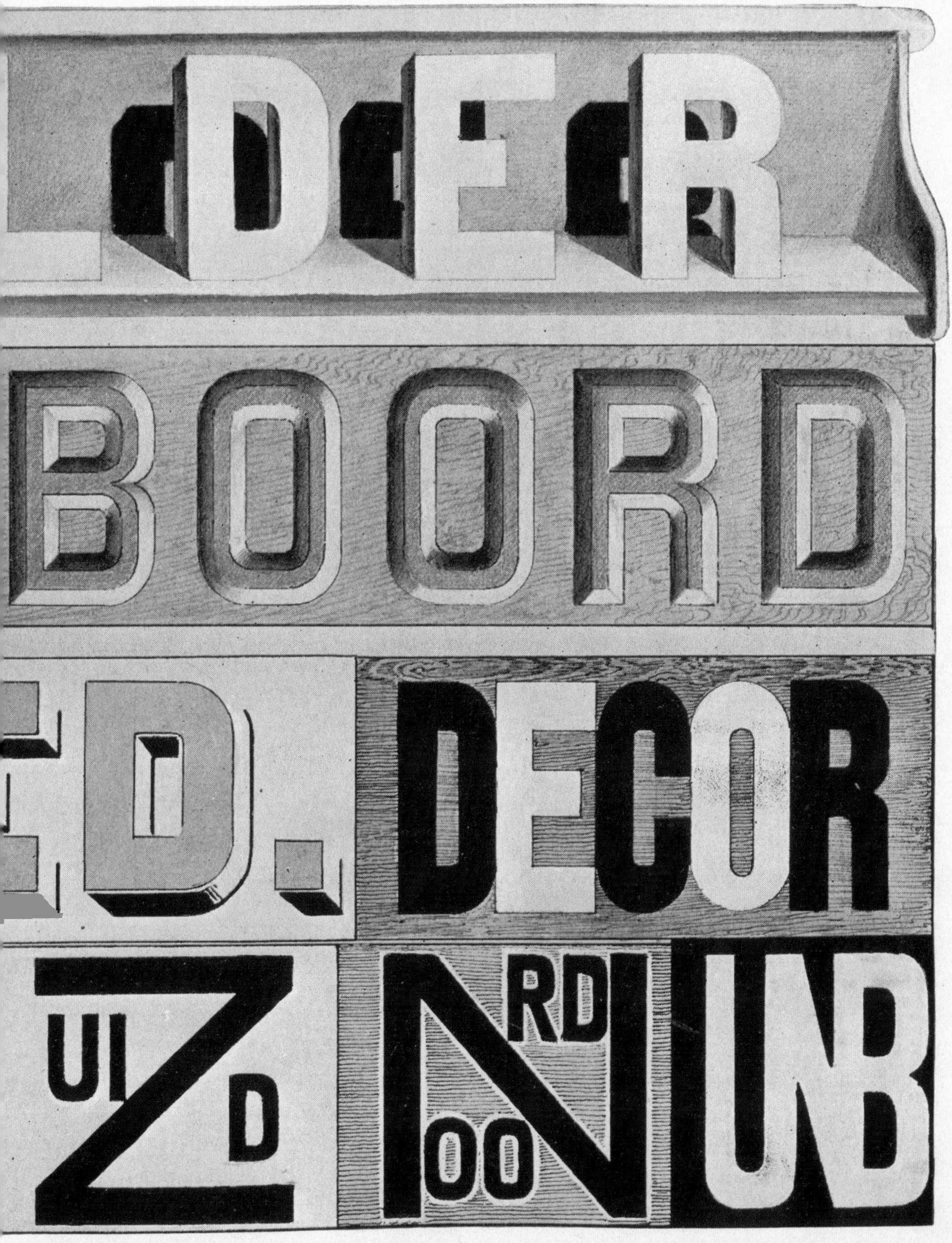
DER
BORD
D.
DECOR
UI
Z
D
RD
N
OO
UB

30-line.   24-line.   20-line.   16-line.   14-line.   12-line.   10-line.

RRRRRRR

Outline, Class 4.

5-line.

CONCERT

8-line.

MACHINES

30-line.   24-line.   20-line.   16-line.   14-line.   12-line.   10-line.

BONDERS

5-line.

CONCERT

8-line.

MACHINES

SONG ROUSED

16-line

MODERNS

BMO AGED

4-line.

PROMENADE

6-line.

Manufactured

149

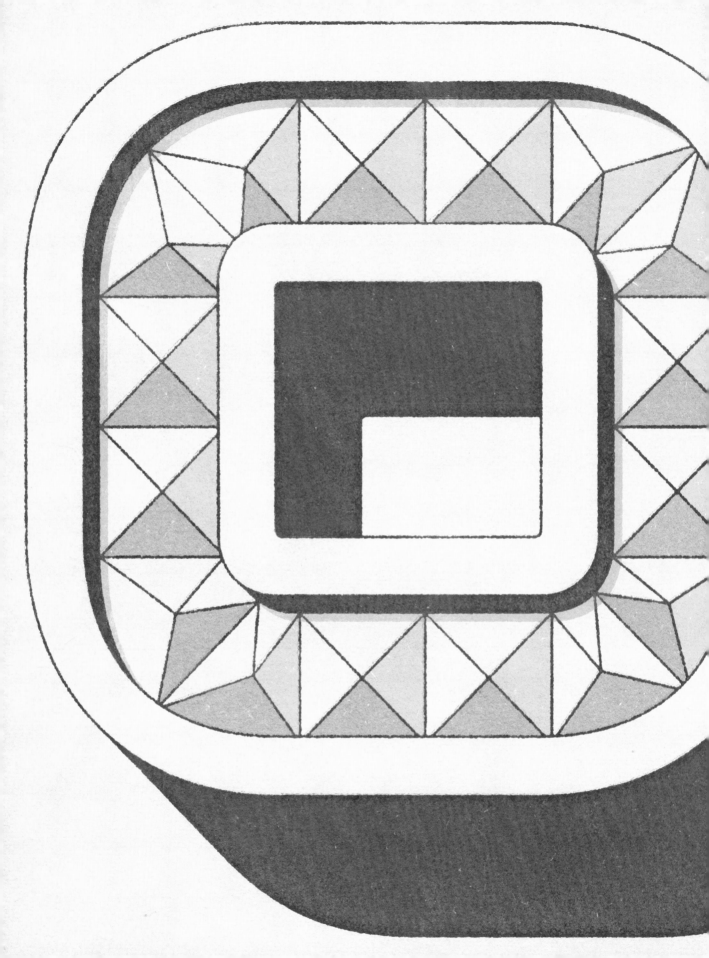

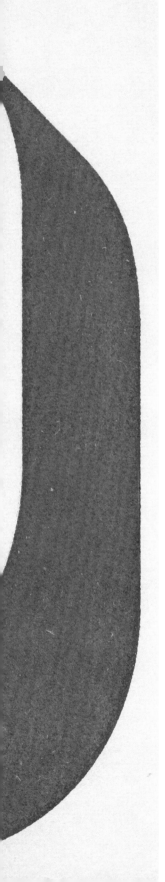

Signs

THERE ARE SIGNS AND THERE ARE SPECTACULAR SIGNS. BIG, BOLD, GRACEFUL, POLISHED, ELABORATE signs whose job was to announce and identify institutions, businesses, individuals, or products. Sign painting was a profitable trade for journeymen and novices. Extensive textbooks, manuals, and elaborate sampler-folios like Albert Schiller's 1890 *Schriften-Schatz, Eine Sammlung Praktischer Alphabete Für Berufszeige Aller Art* (Type Treasure: A Collection of Practical Alphabets for Professional Branches of All Kinds) were bibles of sign making. These specimen groupings are the crème de la crème of the field, yet Germany was only one of many wellsprings for such work. *Artistic Signs: How to Design and Make Them* by E.L. Koller, the director of International Correspondence Schools, produced a less elaborately designed textbook on commercial sign design that addressed a wide range of skills, including the creation of metal, cloth, wire, electric, glass, and relief letter signs, among others. This was a widespread and serious business. Showcard "writers" were among the workhorses of the advertising and identity trade—the pioneers, in a sense, of the graphic designer–typographer. To create these ephemeral cards, designers frequently traced or otherwise copied bold letters from poster type catalogs. Often eye-catching borders were necessary to add allure: "The border demands full consideration in card design," wrote F. A. Pearson in the 1925 edition of *Ticket and Showcard Designing*. "Its effect is that of a frame round a picture. It limits attention within its bounds." In addition, bull's-eyes, stripes, and other geometric patterns guided the viewer's attention to the message.

153

155

A B C D
I J K L T
R S U
GEDOM

F G H V

M N O P

X Y Z

U W R A T B

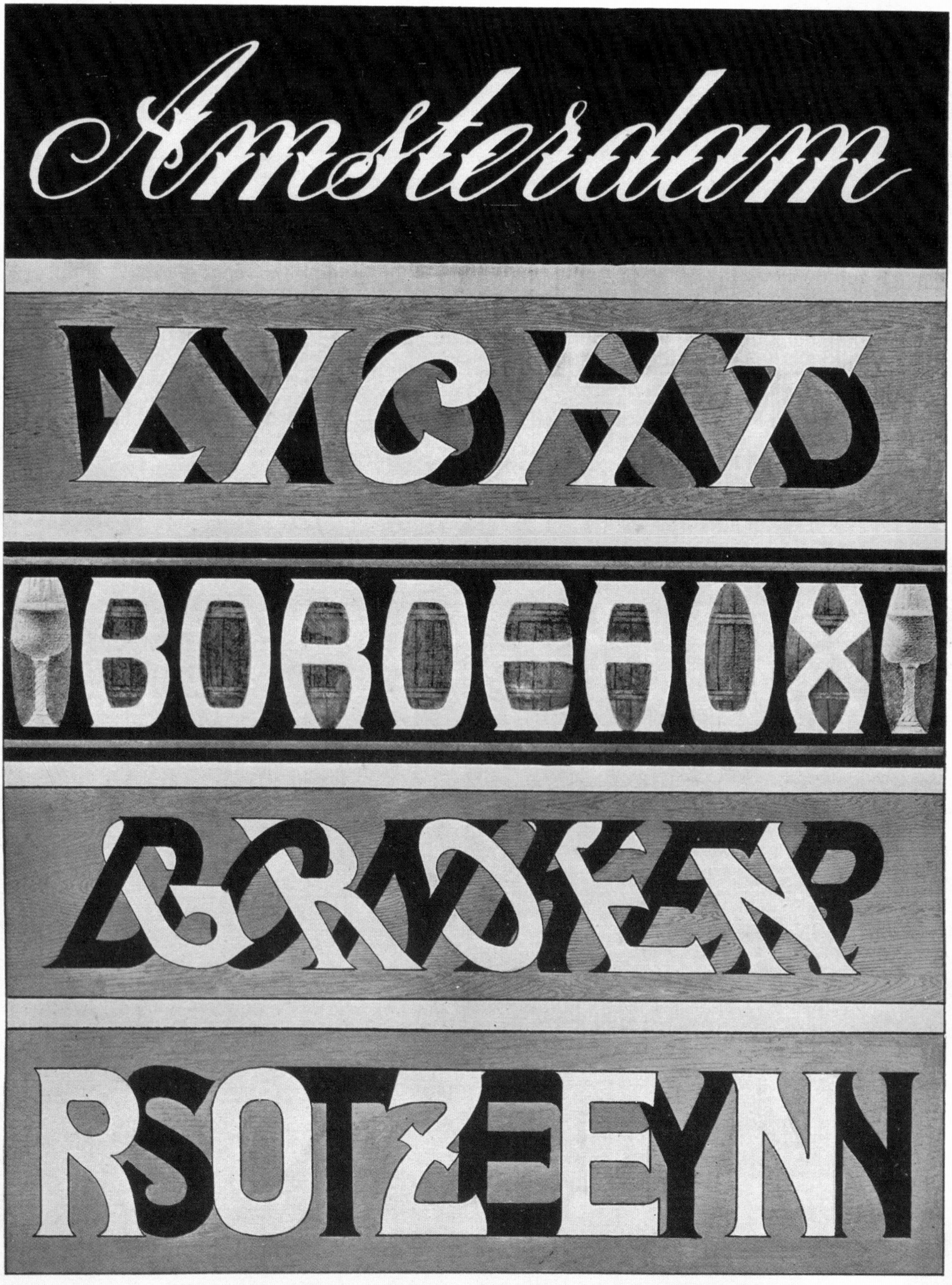
Amsterdam
LICHT
BORDEAUX

G. ROSEN

MODE-HAUS

Kostüm-Atelier.

C. BUER

SPECIAL-SEIDEN HAUS

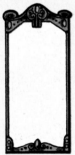

Johann   "ADLER"   Gumper.

DROGEN

ABCD
EFGH
JKLM

abcd
efgh
iklm

NOPR
STUV
WXYZ

nopr
stuv
wxyz

163

E.ARNS

Malermeister.

AUSFÜHRUNG
sämtlicher
Maler-Glaser-
und
Anstreicher
Arbeiten.

Neumann
Berlin
Tabak

ACTIEN
BRAUEREI
ESSEN
BITTER
MÄRZEN
HELL

Atelier
nun für nun
Blumen
Palmen
GEGR
1811.

STERN
BRAUEREI
KRAY.

WEINSTUBE
BERG
1·ETAGE

GIMBORS TINTEN
DIE BESTEN

ABCDEF
GHJKLM

12345

GROSSBUC
GESELLSCH
BERLIN · WIEN · PRAG

BLUMEN-
1.STOCK
KÖRBE

GA
W

789·&

NOPRST
UVWXYZ

HBINDEREI
AFT·M·B·H
PARIS·LONDON·ROM

ALITH
KE

RESTAURATION

HANS KÖLLNES
GEGR.   1903

WALDANDACHT

LONDSE

20-line No. 162.

BON

6-line No. 162.

CUMBERLAND

30-line No. 162.

RD

170

EMPIRE

10 and 16-line No. 246. Cut to any size.

PICTURES

No. 16½ Ends.

HORSE

10 and 14-line No. 247. Cut to any size.

SHOW

Any of these letters can be joined up into blocks when desired.   No. 17 Ends.

HIPPODROME

30-line.

DeLittle's 20-line No. 261HJ.   Classes 2 and 4.

HOD

6-line.

ROUSED

16-line.

DeLittle's 12-line No. 261BJ.   Classes 2 and 4.

AD HEN

6-line.

10-line.

ROUNDS DOG

8-line.

REMINDERS

10-line.

30-line.

14-line.

16-line.

12-line.

The following show how the various 2-colour letters are made up, and their reference numbers :

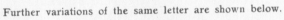

No. 260A.   No. 260B.   No. 260C.   No. 260D.   No. 260E.   No. 260F.   No. 260G.

Class 2.   Class 4.   Class 5.   Class 4.   Class 4.   Class 4.   Class 3.

Further variations of the same letter are shown below.

10-line No. 260EG.

30-line No. 260BG.

14-line 260BG.

16-line No. 260CF.

12-line No. 260CD.

Monograms

A MONOGRAM IS A FAMOUSLY SINUOUS TYPOGRAPHIC PATTERN CREATED BY OVERLAPPING AND INTER- secting two or more letters with or without other graphic motifs to form a single pattern. It is, of course, commonly seen as a personal mark on napkins, handkerchiefs, shirt sleeves, jacket pockets, luggage, and more. This genre of lettering device comes with a lengthy heritage, too: the first is said to have appeared on coins, probably as early as 350 BC. The earliest were the names of the Greek cit- ies that issued the coins, often the first two letters of the city's name. Although many are comprised of and known for decorative and gothic characters with elaborate floral embellishments, monograms have also been devised using more austere sans serif and other modern letter combina- tions and fit into various free-form and geometric shapes. Monograms have been used as dynastic, personal or fam- ily ciphers, signets, crests, insignias, emblems, and badges and have long served as corporate symbols or logos; these are usually made by combining the initials of the individ- ual or the corporation that it represents (a notable exam- ple is the logo for GE, General Electric). Monograms are exquisite typographic gems (the more elaborate, the more jewel-like they are) that demand a designer's keen lettering sensibility and calligraphic facility. They have been used as signatures by artists and craftsmen on all manner of art, pottery, and furniture, on paper, wood, and stone. Some of the examples here are from Max Körner's *Das Neue Monogram und Zeichenwerk* (c. 1950), a sampling of a lost talent, although not a lost art.

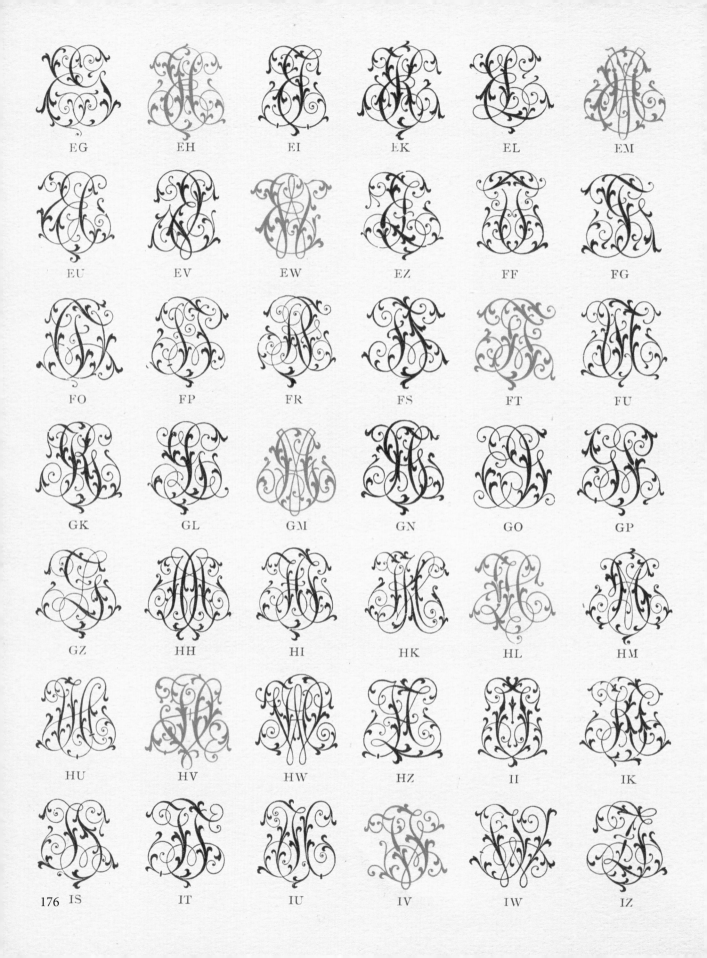

EG EH EI EK EL EM

EU EV EW EZ FF FG

FO FP FR FS FT FU

GK GL GM GN GO GP

GZ HH HI HK HL HM

HU HV HW HZ II IK

IS IT IU IV IW IZ

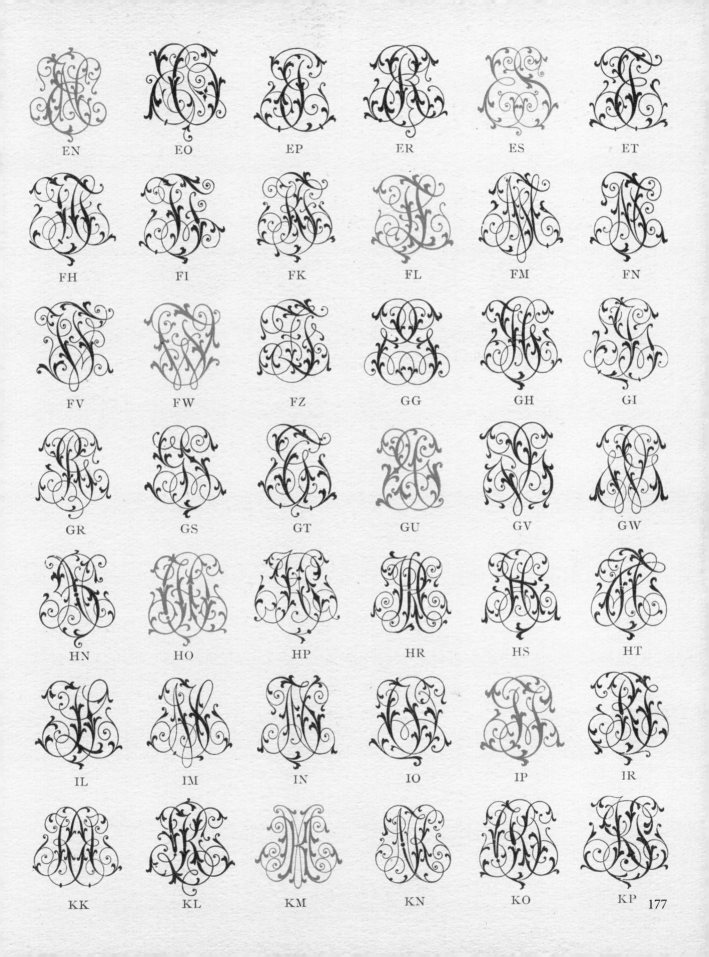

EN   EO   EP   ER   ES   ET

FH   FI   FK   FL   FM   FN

FV   FW   FZ   GG   GH   GI

GR   GS   GT   GU   GV   GW

HN   HO   HP   HR   HS   HT

IL   IM   IN   IO   IP   IR

KK   KL   KM   KN   KO   KP

177

MO	MP	MR	MS	MT	MU	MV
MW	MZ	NN	NO	NP	NR	NS
NT	NU	NV	NW	NZ	OO	OP
OR	OS	OT	OU	OV	OW	OZ
PP	PR	PS	PT	PU	PV	PW
PZ	RR	RS	RT	RU	RV	RW
RZ	SS	ST	SU	SV	SW	SZ

AA   AB   AC   AD   AE   AF

AN   AO   AP   AR   AS   AT

BD   BE   BF   BG   BH   BI

BR   BS   BT   BU   BV   BW

CH   CI   CK   CL   CM   CN

CV   CW   CZ   DD   DE   DF

DN   DO   DP   DR   DS   DT

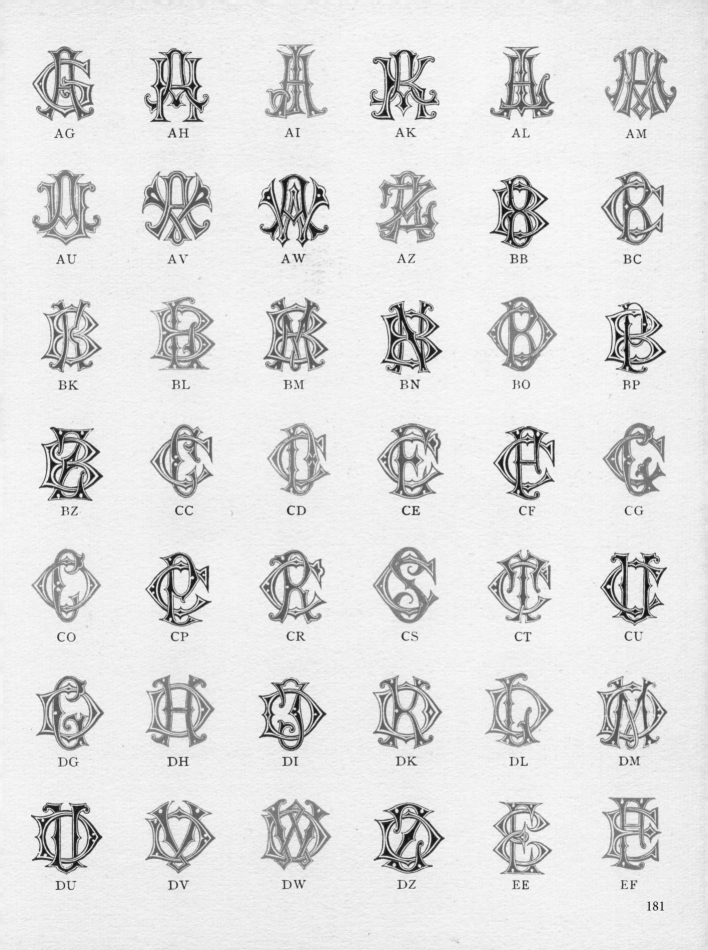

AG	AH	AI	AK	AL	AM
AU	AV	AW	AZ	BB	BC
BK	BL	BM	BN	BO	BP
BZ	CC	CD	CE	CF	CG
CO	CP	CR	CS	CT	CU
DG	DH	DI	DK	DL	DM
DU	DV	DW	DZ	EE	EF

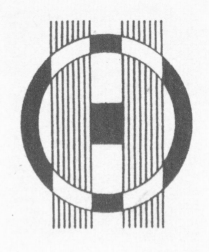

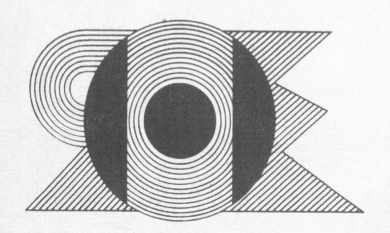

184   R.O.E   G.D.J

R.E.O

b.P.O

R.T.V

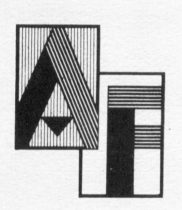

186

A.E.O.V

O.M

187

188

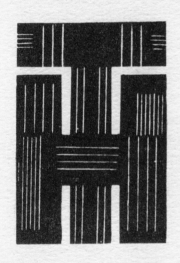

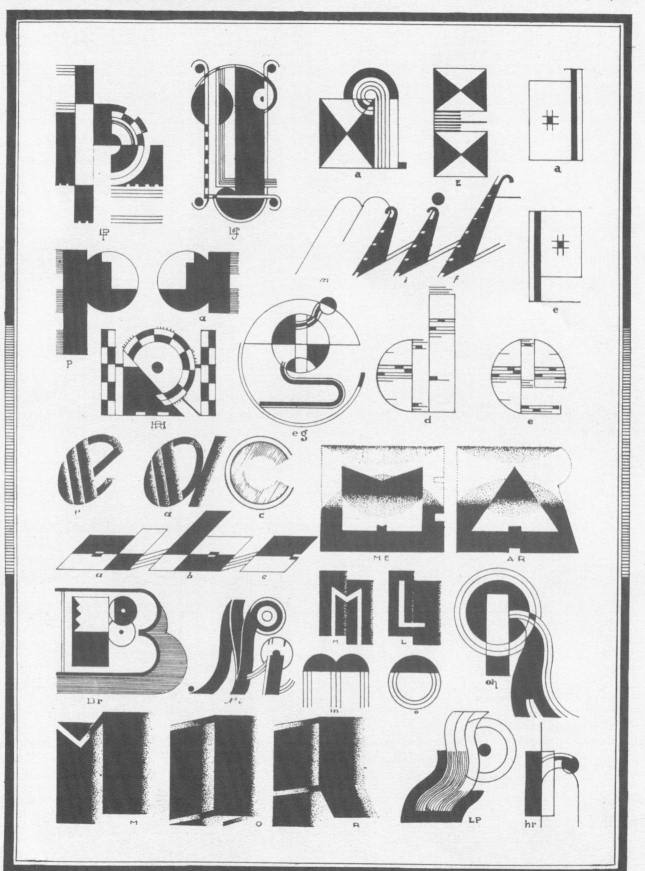

N° 1

N° 2

N° 3

N° 4

N° 6

N° 8

N° 9

N° 5

N° 7

N° 10

Albert Schiller's Schriften-Schatz, Eine Sammlung Praktischer Alphabete Für Berufszeige Aller Art. Otto Maier, Ravensburg, Germany. 1890.
Pages ii–iii, 3–60, 131–140

Alphabets Nouveaux, 200 alphabets et chiffres pour draps, taies, nappes, serviettes, lingerie. Editions A. Ponchon, collection Bleuet, Paris, France. 1935.
Pages 193–194

Cutalogs of Type Warmers from Cobb Shinn. Conrad X. Shinn, Indianapolis, IN. Date unknown.
Pages 119–124

DeLittle's Wood Letter Specimens. R. D. DeLittle, York, England. 1923.
Pages 91–92, 101–102, 107–108, 149–150, 171–174

Farbige Alphabete: 55 Tafeln Sammelmappe. Otto Heim, Niedersedlitz-Dresden, Germany. 1925.
Page 142

H. Berthold Gesellschaft m. b. H., Vienna, Austria. Date unknown.
Pages 111, 141

Jolies lettres: Album contenant des modèles d'alphabets et de monogrammes pour la lingerie et le linge de maison. Mme J. Sonrel, Paris, France. 1958.
Pages 115–116

Kaemmerer's Practical Letter Book. J. H. Kaemmerer, London, England. 1911.
Pages 99–100, 109–110, 143–148, 155–159, 161–162

Lettres Brodées: Album contenant des modèles d'alphabets et de monogrammes pour la lingerie et le linge de maison. Mme J. Sonrel, Paris, France. 1953.
Pages 113–114

Lettres et Chiffres Modernes Inédits; Chiffres, Monogrammes et Rehauts Modernes. Les Éditions Guérinet, R. Panzani, Paris, France. Date unknown. Pages 61–64, 185–188, 191–192

Modern Lettering Design and Application, William Helburn, New York, NY, c. 1921. Pages 189–190

Neue-Scfhriften Firmenschilder, Kungewerbe Verlag, Gerhard & Co., Essen, Germany. 1905. Pages 93–94, 103–106, 153–154, 160, 163–170

Primary Quarterly. The American Sunday School Union, Philadelphia, PA. 1893. Page 98

Printer's sample book (original pasted in labels), unpublished c. 1935. (Author's private collection.) Pages 125–128

Schriften Atlas. Eine Sammlung der wchtigsten Schreib-und Druckschriften aus alter und neuer Zeit nebst Initialen, Monogrammen, Wappen, Landesfarben und heraldischen Motiven, für die praktischen Zwecke des Kunstgewerbes. Ludwig Petzendorfer, Julius Hoffmann, Stuttgart, Germany. 1898. Pages 177–182

Schriften Atlas Neue Folge. Eine Sammlung von Alphabeten Initialen und Monogrammen. Ludwig Petzendorfer, Julius Hoffmann, Stuttgart, Germany. 1905. Pages 67–70, 73–82, 97

Spécimen Général de La Fonderie Typographique Française. Société Anonyme, Paris. Date unknown. Pages 71–72, 83–90, 112

BOOKS FROM ALLWORTH PRESS

ABOUT DESIGN
by Gordon Salchow, foreword by Michael Bierut, afterword by Katherine McCoy (6⅛ × 6⅛, 208 pages, paperback, $19.99)

ADVERTISING DESIGN AND TYPOGRAPHY
by Alex W. White (8½ × 11, 224 pages, paperback, $29.99)

CITIZEN DESIGNER (SECOND EDITION)
by Steven Heller and Véronique Vienne (6 × 9, 312 pages, paperback, $22.99)

DESIGN LITERACY
by Steven Heller with Rick Poynor (6 × 9, 304 pages, paperback, $22.50)

DESIGN THINKING
by Thomas Lockwood (6 × 9, 304 pages, paperback, $24.95)

THE EDUCATION OF A GRAPHIC DESIGNER
by Steven Heller (6 × 9, 380 pages, paperback, $19.99)

THE ELEMENTS OF LOGO DESIGN
by Alex W. White (8 × 10, 224 pages, paperback, $24.99)

GRAPHIC DESIGN RANTS & RAVES
by Steven Heller (7 × 9, 200 pages, paperback, $19.99)

GREEN GRAPHIC DESIGN
by Brian Dougherty with Celery Design Collaborative (6 × 9, 212 pages, paperback, $24.95)

HOW TO THINK LIKE A GREAT GRAPHIC DESIGNER
by Debbie Millman (6 × 9, 248 pages, paperback, $24.95)

LOOKING CLOSER 5: CRITICAL WRITINGS ON GRAPHIC DESIGN
Edited by Michael Bierut, William Drenttel, and Steven Heller (6¾ × 9¾, 256 pages, paperback, $21.95)

THE SWASTIKA AND SYMBOLS OF HATE
by Steven Heller (6 × 9, 216 pages, hardcover, $24.99)

TEACHING GRAPHIC DESIGN (SECOND EDITION)
by Steven Heller (6 × 9, 312 pages, paperback, $24.99)

TEACHING GRAPHIC DESIGN HISTORY
by Steven Heller (6 × 9, 312 pages, paperback, $24.99)

VINTAGE TYPE AND GRAPHICS
by Steven Heller and Louise Fili (7½ × 9⅛, 208 pages, paperback, $17.95)

To see our complete catalog or to order online, please visit www.allworth.com.